SKILLS IN
RELIGIOUS
STUDIES

Book 2

S C MERCIER WITH J FAGEANT

Heinemann Educational Publishers
Halley Court, Jordan Hill, Oxford OX2 8EJ
a division of Reed Educational & Professional Publishing Ltd

OXFORD   FLORENCE   PRAGUE   MADRID   ATHENS
MELBOURNE   AUCKLAND   KUALA LUMPUR   SINGAPORE
TOKYO   IBADAN   NAIROBI   KAMPALA   JOHANNESBURG
GABORONE   PORTSMOUTH NH (USA)   CHICAGO
MEXICO CITY   SAO PAULO

Heinemann is a registered trademark of Reed Educational &
Professional Publishing Ltd

Text © J Fageant and S C Mercier, 1989, 1998

First published 1989
This edition published 1998

02 01 00 99 98
10 9 8 7 6 5 4 3 2 1

British Library Cataloguing in Publication Data
A catalogue record for this book is available from the
British Library

ISBN 0 435 30204 3

Designed and typeset by Ken Vail Graphic Design, Cambridge
Picture research by Jacqui Rivers
Cover designed by Aricot Vert
Printed and bound in Great Britain by Bath Colourbooks, Glasgow

Acknowledgements
The publishers would like to thank the following for
permission to reproduce copyright material.
Scriptures quoted from the *Good News Bible* published
by the Bible Societies/HarperCollins Publishers Ltd.,
UK, © American Bible Society, 1966, 1971, 1976, 1992;
'The Teaching of Buddha' © 1996 by Bukkyo Dendo
Kyokai, Buddhist Promoting Foundation, 3-14, 4-
chome, Shiba, Minato-ku, Tokyo, Japan, 108, 137th
revised ed., 1987 on p. 47; The cover design from *Faith
in the City: The Report of the Archbishop of
Canterbury's Commission on Urban Priority Areas*
(Church House Publishing, 1985) is copyright The
Central Board of Finance of the Church of England and
is reproduced by permission on p. 63; The text of the
Nicene Creed (adapted) as it appears in the Order for
Holy Communion Rite A in *The Alternative Service
Book* 1980 on p. 48 is copyright © 1970, 1971, 1975
International Consultation on English Texts (ICET).
The Lord's Prayer in its modern form is adapted from
the ICET version on p. 61; Manchester University Press
for the extracts from *Textual sources for the study of
Sikhism* on pp. 85 and 88; The Muslim Educational
Trust for the translated quotations of the Qur'an from
Islam: Beliefs and Teachings by Ghulam Sarwar on pp.
64 and 66; Poster produced and published by Ta-Ha
Publishers Ltd. on p. 66; World Council of Churches,
150 Route de Ferney, 1211 Geneva 2, Switzerland for
the badge on p. 55.

The publishers would like to thank the following for
permission to use photographs.
A.K.G. on p. 52; Mark Azavedo on pp. 25, 43, 46, 56,
73, 74; Circa photo library on pp. 6, 7, 8, 11, 22, 23, 26,
28, 31, 34, 41, 44, 48, 55, 59, 68, 70, 78, 92; Garden
Matters on pp. 34, 47; Hutchison Photo Library on pp.
20, 38, 50, 65, 79, 93; Impact Photo Library on pp. 6, 8,
16, 63, 65, 73, 88; Metropolitan Police on p. 5;
Christine Osborne on pp. 28, 39, 40, 53, 59, 61, 83, 86;
Peter Sanders on p. 66; Science Photo Library on p. 4;
Skyscan on p. 49; Travel Ink on p. 46; Trip on pp. 4, 10,
12, 13, 14, 20, 21, 29, 30, 35, 36, 37, 44, 45, 50, 54, 57,
64, 67, 69, 71, 73, 75, 76, 77, 79, 80, 82, 84, 85, 86, 87,
90, 91; Tropix Photo Library on p. 76.

The publishers would like to thank Impact/Mohamed
Ansar, James Davis Worldwide, Peter Sanders and
Andes Press Agency/Carlos Reyes-Manzo
for permission to reproduce the cover photographs.

The publishers have made every effort to trace
copyright holders. However, if any material has been
incorrectly acknowledged, we would be pleased to
correct this at the earliest opportunity.

Contents

1 Faith and authority

There are some important decisions and choices that everyone has to face in life and there are some difficult questions to answer. For example, at some point we have to face the questions: 'How should I live my life?' 'What are the rules?' 'What are my responsibilities to other people?' 'Is there a way of knowing what is right and what is wrong?' Some people say you are on your own. You have to work it out for yourself. Others simply follow the crowd. Those who belong to a religious faith say that we are not alone in our search for answers to these questions. They believe that there are signposts to help us on our way in life. And there are guidelines that have been tried and tested by people before us.

B *Does the voice of science carry greater authority than the voice of religion today?*

Sometimes these guidelines appear as a set of laws or teachings. For example, there are the Ten Commandments in the Jewish **Torah** and the **Eightfold Path** in Buddhism. Sometimes the guidance is given through the example of great leaders and teachers. Sikhs follow the example of the Ten Gurus and Muslims look for guidance in the life and example of **Muhammad**. Sometimes the guidance comes in the form of stories. For example, the parables of Jesus help Christians make decisions about how to live and the stories from the Hindu scriptures influence the lives of Hindus today.

Many of the religious stories, teachings and traditions passed down through the ages are contained in the sacred writings of the faiths. These scriptures have a special authority for the followers of the different faiths. The believers find in them wisdom and truth. They also discover that if they follow the guidance given then they find support, reassurance and peace. It is partly this experience that gives the tradition its authority.

A *Do our religious leaders still carry authority?*

For many people, it is the teachings and traditions of their faith that they turn to when they come up against the difficult questions of life. Religious teachings do not contain easy answers. Sometimes their advice is hard to swallow. They do offer alternatives to a life based on selfishness, indecision, greed or fear.

The word of scripture still holds authority for many people

Discussion question

What voices of authority do people listen to today? Look at the photos to help you, and think of some of your own. Why do you think people accept the authority of these voices?

At the heart of each religion is the belief that the truth has been revealed or given to humankind. In other words, the truth is eternal and not merely the invention of men and women. In some religious traditions it is God who decides to reveal the truth to people. This is why scriptures are considered sacred and treated with respect. The teachings they contain carry the authority of God's word.

THINGS TO DO

1 Divide a page into sections. Draw a cartoon or symbol to represent the different voices of authority which people listen to. In each case explain why people accept that authority, e.g. the authority of science, of the law, of teachers, of political leaders, of peer group opinion, of the media, etc.

2 People might say that some rules for living are 'just true', you cannot prove them, you just have to accept them as given truths. For example, you should not kill, you should not steal, etc. Make up a list of six 'given truths'. Compare yours with those of others in the class. Put together an agreed class list. What reasons or arguments can you give for the truth of these rules and guidelines for living? What makes them true?

3 What are the things that humans need most help with in the world today – poverty, war, the destruction of the environment? Imagine the world is sending a message in a bottle – out into the universe. Write the message, asking for guidance and help to put things right. Say how you would like the message to be answered.

4 Science is regarded as an important authority in the world today. What does it have to say on some of the following questions and issues – how the universe came into being, how life began on earth, climate change, and the causes of illness and disease? What alternative theories have existed in the past that still exist today? What gives science its authority? What are the difficult questions in life on which science has little to say? Discuss these questions in class, then write up your own answers.

2 Hinduism: Gurus and sacred texts

Hinduism is a rich and varied religion. It cannot be summed up in a set of unified beliefs and practices. It has no single founder. However, there is a long tradition of spiritual teachers. There is not one holy book but several collections of sacred writings. Spiritual truth can be revealed in different forms and Hindus recognize the authority of the saint or spiritual teacher as well as the words of sacred texts which carry the authority of God.

Many Hindus follow the teachings of a **guru** or spiritual teacher. For example, Sathya Sai Baba (**A**) has a large following in both India and the UK. His teachings are based on the principles of love, truth, peace and not harming. Other Hindus belong to the **Krishna Consciousness Movement** and look to the example and teachings of the Bengali saint Chaitanya who taught his followers to accept Krishna as the Supreme Lord. More recently his teachings have been brought to the West by A.C. Bhaktivedanta Swami.

Discussion question

What do you understand by the term spiritual teacher? In what way are they different from other teachers?

The Hindu scriptures are communicated in a variety of ways (**B**). Words from the scriptures are recited every day in worship at the **shrine** and temple. Travelling theatre groups and storytellers keep the ancient religious traditions alive. Some of the scriptures are in the ancient Indian language of Sanskrit. Hindus can read their words in translation. Children get to know the stories from comic-strip books and many now watch versions on film and video.

There are two main groups of scripture in the Hindu tradition. One is called **Shruti**, which means 'revealed'. Hindus believe that these were revealed to the holy men of ancient

A *Sathya Sai Baba has many followers in India and the UK*

B *Words from the Hindu scriptures are used in worship and in teaching*

ndia. This group of writings includes the Vedas and **Upanishads**, the most ancient and most sacred of the Hindu scriptures. The Vedas contain hymns and prayers still used in worship today. The Upanishads are concerned with questions about **atman**, the human soul, and **Brahman**, the Supreme Spirit. The word Upanishad means 'to sit down near'. The holy men of ancient India passed on these words to their students who sat next to them and listened to their teachings.

C *For some Gandhi is a divine figure and his image is revered*

There is another group of scriptures called **Smriti**, which means 'remembered'. These contain the famous and well-loved epics of the **Mahabharata** and the **Ramayana**. They are full of moral and spiritual guidance. Perhaps the best known of the Smriti texts is the **Bhagavad Gita**, which means the 'Song of the Lord'. It is a part of the Mahabharata and contains the words of Lord **Krishna**. The **Puranas**, which contain stories about the various Hindu deities, belong within the Smriti tradition. The **Laws of Manu** which give Hindus guidance on how to live at each stage in life are also considered sacred scripture.

THINGS TO DO

1 Divide a page into two columns with the headings Shruti and Smriti. Under each heading explain the characteristics of the two different groups of Hindu scriptures. Describe them and say what they contain.

2 Look at photo **B**. What can you see? How can you tell that these are sacred scriptures? Write an interview with a Hindu priest in which you put these questions. Include some questions of your own and write the answers the priest gives.

3 A sacred text can be a symbol of truth and so it is treated with respect. If you were allowed to keep only one book for life, which book would it be? What would it represent for you? How would you make sure that it was preserved safely and treated with care and respect? Explain your answer in writing.

4 As well as being a great political leader Gandhi is often seen as a spiritual teacher. He helped India in her struggle for independence and showed the world the way of non-violence. Images of Gandhi are seen in shrines and his teachings are regarded as important today (**C**). Think of someone today who represents truth or peace or some other important message for the world. Design a poster or icon of the person you have chosen and explain why you have chosen them.

What is real?

The Hindu scriptures (**A**) explore some of the deep and difficult questions of life. For example, 'What is real?', 'What is lasting?', 'What can we rely on?' Someone could point to a house and say that is real. But in a few years it may be knocked down and become a heap of rubble. A house has no lasting reality. A person could touch the ground and say it is real, but one day even the earth will come to an end. All things change. All things pass. Nothing that we see or touch, taste or smell will remain forever.

Discussion question

Do you think that anything remains the same? Is there anything that has lasting substance or reality?

According to the Hindu scriptures, there is only one thing that is lasting and real. Only Brahman is real. Everything else is **maya**. Maya is the world of things that have no lasting reality. Brahman is the Supreme Spirit. Brahman is eternal and unchanging.

A *The Hindu scriptures are looked to for answers to life's questions*

When everything else is dissolved or destroyed, Brahman will remain. Brahman is everywhere and within everything.

There is a story in the Upanishads about a student who wants to understand the nature of Brahman (**B**). His guru tells him to take some salt and put it in a bowl of water. Later there is no sign of the salt. Then the guru asks his student to sip the water from one side of the bowl, then from the other. From every side he can taste the salt. So it is with Brahman – although Brahman cannot be seen it can be perceived everywhere and in everything.

B *Teachers and gurus explain the meaning of life*

Samsara – the never-ending cycle of rebirth

For Hindus, Brahman is present in every living creature. According to the Hindu scriptures, every living creature has a soul. Hindus call the soul atman. Many Hindus say the soul is Brahman. Since the soul is Brahman it is also eternal. When the body dies the soul lives on. It takes on another body and is born again into the world. The cycle of birth, life, death and rebirth is called **samsara (C)**.

Hindus believe that the quality of our next life depends on how we act in this life. Every action we carry out has an effect on us. It leaves its mark. This is the law of **karma**. Karma means actions and the effects of actions. If our actions are good, we are rewarded. If our actions are selfish or evil, we pay for them. So we build up karma every time we act. Karma acts like a fuel – it drives us on into the next existence, and the next. We are caught in a never-ending cycle of birth, death and rebirth. The Hindu scriptures offer guidance on how to escape from this cycle. Release from this continual process of birth and death is called **moksha**. Once the soul is released from the cycle of karma and samsara it is united with God (Brahman).

THINGS TO DO

1 Tell the story of the guru and his student in words and pictures. Make sure you explain the meaning of the story.

2 Does everything we do have an effect on us? Do we become what our actions make us? Which actions have the most effect? Divide a page in two. On one side list actions that might have a positive effect on our character. On the other write down those actions which have a negative effect on us. Compare your lists with those of a partner.

3 Represent the cycle of rebirth in a picture or diagram. You need to show the following ideas:
   • birth is followed by life, death and rebirth
   • every life is linked to the next
   • the cycle is never-ending.

4 People have often wondered 'Is this world we experience real?', 'What if it is just all in our heads?' Hindus believe it is not as real nor as important as we make it out to be. We behave as if it were lasting reality but it will all pass away. What are your thoughts on this? Write a poem or a diary entry in which you explore these questions.

Aims for living

The Hindu scriptures describe four aims in life. One is to create prosperity which is called **artha** (A). People want to make money. They want to provide for their family and live in comfort. Some people enjoy the challenge of creating prosperity. According to Hindu tradition, this can be a respectable aim in life. A successful person can help build the wealth of the community. However, in the long run, success in this area will not guarantee real happiness or peace of mind.

Another aim in life is sense enjoyment, called **kama**. According to Hindu tradition, physical love is not to be taken lightly. It is way of giving and receiving pleasure. It can bring great joy and it is a gift from God. Hindus believe that wanting to share a loving, sexual relationship within marriage is a valid aim in life. However, it cannot give lasting peace or happiness.

A *Lakshmi is the goddess of wealth and prosperity. Hindus pray to Lakshmi to ask for success and prosperity*

All these aims are important and have their place. However, the ultimate goal in life for most Hindus is moksha. Moksha is release from karma and samsara. The Hindu scriptures say karma is the result of action but we act because we want, like or hate. It is therefore the desires and intentions behind our actions which generate karma. If we could stop the longing, the wanting, the hating, then we would stop accumulating karma.

Some Hindus choose to give up the comforts and ties of the material life in order to become free from the bonds of karma (**B**). Through **asceticism**, **meditation** and **yoga** they burn up the accumulated karma. Yoga is an ancient system of exercises for controlling the thoughts and senses. This path of self-discipline begins with truthfulness, gentleness and respect for all life. Once all past karma has been burned up, at death the soul is released and finds union with God.

B *Some Hindus give up the comforts of life*

Discussion question

How do the aims of artha and kama compare with your aims in life?

Another aim in life is **dharma**, which means religion or religious duty (see unit 5). A person who fulfils their dharma in life looks after their own moral and spiritual development and cares for the needs of others. A person's dharma depends on their position in society and on their stage in life. For example, it is the duty (dharma) of parents to support and care for their family.

THINGS TO DO

1 Design a poster or collage to illustrate the Hindu aims in life.
2 Write a letter to a Hindu friend explaining your four aims in life. Then write a letter in response from your friend explaining the four aims in life from a Hindu point of view.
3 Hindus believe that doing 'what you are meant to do', i.e. doing what is right, ensures the future well-being of yourself and others. It is a student's duty to work hard at their studies. This may lead to opportunities in the future so that they will be able to find work and support others. Suggest three more examples that would illustrate this belief. Write your own thoughts on the value of doing 'what you are meant to do'.
4 Every action we make has a desire or intention behind it. Every action has an effect on the person who acts. Illustrate the truth of these two points in a story or in a short script for a play.

5 Duty and righteousness

Dharma means religion, law or duty or doing what is right. It refers to the laws that govern the universe as well as the duties of each individual. The best loved teaching on dharma is the story of Rama. Hindus worship Rama as an **avatar** of the god **Vishnu**. Avatar means 'one who comes down'. In other words, God came down to earth as Rama.

Long ago, in India, there lived a prince called Rama. He was an obedient son and heir to his father's throne. His father, the king, had promised his wife, the queen, two wishes. Envious of Rama's position, she demanded that he be exiled for fourteen years in the forest and that her son be crowned

instead. The old king kept his promise but died broken-hearted. Rama knew it was his duty to keep the promise made by his father even though everyone wanted to make him king. So he went into exile.

In the forest, Rama's wife, Sita, was kidnapped by the demon, Ravana. This evil tyrant threatened the peace of the world. Rama rescued Sita and destroyed the tyrant. After fourteen years Rama returned to be crowned (**A**). As ruler and king it was Rama's duty to establish peace and justice in his kingdom. Throughout his reign Rama put his people's welfare before his own and was obedient to his dharma.

According to the Hindu scriptures, a person's dharma depends on their position in society. Traditionally, there were four main divisions in Hindu society. These are called **varnas**. There is a story in the Hindu scriptures in which the four varnas come from the mouth, arms, legs and feet of a mighty giant. From his mouth came the **Brahmin** class, the priests and teachers. From his arms came the **Kshatriyas**, the rulers and warriors. His thighs became the **Vaishyas**, those in business, farming or trade. From the feet came the **Shudra** class, the servants, craftsmen and labourers.

A *Rama and his wife Sita represent the importance of dharma*

Discussion question

What do you think is the duty of:
- *a parent*
- *a political leader*
- *a doctor*
- *a teacher*
- *a shopkeeper*
- *a cleaner?*

The scriptures give detailed guidance on the duty, or dharma, of each class. When each class fulfils its dharma, society runs smoothly and the needs of everyone are served.

Other groups grew up within the main classes. These are known as **jati** or castes and they were related to occupation. Some

B Those who were once called outcastes now prefer the term dalit or the oppressed – why?

jobs were believed to be unclean. People in these occupations were considered outcastes or **untouchables**. In the past they could not enjoy the rights enjoyed by others. Today it is illegal to discriminate against outcastes. However, prejudices against them remain and they call themselves the 'dalit' or the oppressed (**B**).

THINGS TO DO

1 Rama is a model of dharma or righteousness. Doing what is right often means making a personal sacrifice. Tell the story of Rama and explain how it demonstrates the meaning of dharma.

2 Draw a diagram to represent the four varnas. Underneath explain what you think the duty or dharma of each would be. Compare your answers with those of a partner. Discuss the answers in class.

3 When everyone does what is right and fulfils their duty then the needs of everyone are served (**C**). Does this rule work? Write a story to illustrate this idea set in the context of your school or in the context of your home and family.

4 All societies have their divisions. Some are helpful, some are not. How is our society divided? Which divisions are helpful and which lead to the rights of people being ignored? Give your answer in the form of a newspaper article.

C The dharma of the teacher is to enlighten his or her students

The song of the Lord

One of the best loved of the Hindu scriptures is the Mahabharata. This is a poem about a war between two royal families, the Pandavas, or sons of Pandu, and their cousins the Kauravas.

There was once a king called Pandu who gave up his throne to go in search of moksha. He asked his brother to act as king and to be like a father to his sons. His brother agreed. However, his sons became jealous of the Pandavas. They robbed them of their inheritance and tricked them out of their land. The Pandavas tried to recover what was rightly theirs. Having tried all peaceful means to establish a just settlement, the sons of Pandu were forced into battle against their cousins.

One of the Pandavas, **Arjuna**, was a skilled and courageous warrior. As the battle lines were drawn up, Arjuna was filled with horror at the thought of shedding the blood of his

A *Krishna teaching Arjuna*

own family. He turned to his charioteer, Krishna, and asked him what he should do. Krishna told Arjuna to fight. It was his duty as a prince and warrior to fight against evil and establish justice. Krishna reminded Arjuna that he would not be killing the souls but only the bodies of those he slayed.

Krishna told Arjuna that he must go to battle without any selfish intention or desire. He must fight without any feelings of envy or hatred or personal desire for power. In this way he would not accumulate bad karma. He must be detached from the outcome of the battle and fight for what is right and not for himself.

Discussion question

Is it possible to act without any selfish desires or intentions? Why would it be difficult to do this?

In the course of this discussion, Krishna reveals that he is the Supreme Lord God. This discourse is called the Bhagavad Gita, the Song of the Lord (**A**). In it Krishna tells Arjuna of the three ways to moksha. The first way is **jnana yoga**, the way of knowledge. It requires giving up all possessions and personal ties. It calls for a life of meditation, yoga and asceticism (see page 11). In this way it is possible to burn up the past karma which stands in the way of moksha.

Another way to moksha that Krishna teaches is the way of unselfish action or **karma yoga**. There is no need to give up a life of action. However, every action must be carried out without any selfish desire or intention (**B**). It means having no attachment to the results of actions. In this way no karma follows from the action and the soul is free from the chains of samsara and will not be reborn.

The third way to moksha is the way of loving devotion (bhakti yoga). This is explained in the next unit.

B *Those working in this leper rehabilitation centre in India are following the path of unselfish action*

THINGS TO DO

1 In your own words, tell the story that leads up to the teachings of the Bhagavad Gita and explain why Krishna has to give Arjuna a talk before battle.
2 Krishna tells Arjuna he must fight. Write up his advice in the form of a comic strip for children to read. Make sure you cover the main points of his argument.
3 Many would say that the way of jnana yoga is more difficult than that of karma yoga. Describe each of these ways to moksha and say which you think would be the more difficult. Give your reasons.
4 'Do your best but do not desire the outcome and do not seek personal gain.' Try to live by this teaching for a day. Write about the experience and say what you learnt from it.

7 The way of love

Discussion question

What are the ways in which people express their love and devotion when they are truly in love?

In the Bhagavad Gita, Lord Krishna offers a third way to attain moksha. **Bhakti yoga** is the way of loving devotion. It means loving God in body, mind and spirit. Every action becomes an act of devotion to God and all desire is focused on pleasing God. Krishna calls his devotees to love and serve him and in turn he promises to release them from the chains of karma and samsara.

The way of bhakti yoga encourages the worshipper to see God as a lover or beloved. Someone who is in love thinks about the object of their love all the time. They may give presents or sing love songs. So Hindus express their love for God through offerings, acts of devotion and song.

Some Hindus recite the many names of God as an act of loving devotion. Followers of the Krishna Consciousness Movement (**A**) chant the names of Rama and Krishna, the two main avatars of Vishnu. They believe that this can help purify the heart and mind filling it with devotion and the consciousness of God's presence.

Many Hindus express their love and devotion through worship at a shrine (**B**). Most Hindus have a shrine in the home and the day often begins with an act of devotion. For example, if the mother rises first, she showers and dresses in clean clothes but does not put on shoes. Then she approaches the shrine and bows before the **deity**. She

A *Members of the Krishna Consciousness Movement sing their love for Krishna*

B *Hindus worship in the home with offerings of food*

may ring a bell as one would on entering someone's house. She then washes the image of the deity and offers **incense**. Offerings of flowers, water and food are set before the deity and a **ghee lamp** is lit and moved reverently before the form of the deity. The mother may recite hymns and prayers and call on God to help her through the day.

In the evening the family may gather for worship before they eat together. Offerings of food from the meal are set before the deity. It is then blessed and returned to the table and the meal becomes blessed food. In a Hindu home the food is generally vegetarian. Hindus believe that all living creatures have a soul. Animals are therefore treated with respect and not killed for food.

Many Hindus practise meditation each day. Some use yoga exercises to help them control and quieten the body and mind. Others may sit before the shrine and focus on the form of the deity. Singing bhajans (hymns) or reciting **mantras** (prayers) are also ways of meditating on God.

THINGS TO DO

1 Design a poster or diagram to illustrate the three yogas – jnana yoga, karma yoga and bhakti yoga. You will need to refer back to unit 6 to help you. Explain your design in writing.

2 In what ways is the path of bhakti yoga similar to being in love? Write an interview script on bhakti yoga in which you put this question to a Krishna devotee. Include some questions of your own, too, and write the answers given by the Krishna devotee.

3 Prepare a leaflet on 'The Hindu home' which could be given to social workers with no knowledge or understanding of Hinduism. Make sure that the information encourages respect and understanding for the Hindu way of life.

4 Worship at the shrine is the outward expression of love. It is the inward love and devotion that really matters. What actions and aspects of your life are only outward expressions of something much deeper? Describe an example from your own experience.

8 The temple

The Hindu temple is called a **mandir**. In India, a mandir is essentially the house of a deity (**A**). There is usually a priest to take care of the shrine which contains an image of the deity. Worshippers go to the temple just as they might go to visit a close friend. They stop to pray, to make an offering or to express their devotion by walking reverently around the shrine. The temple buildings can be very elaborate or very simple. At some temples the roof over the central shrine is built high to represent the Himalayas, the traditional home of the gods.

In the UK, the mandir may be in a converted building or it may be purpose-built. There is a shrine room with a prayer hall large enough to take a congregation. In the UK, the mandir may have several shrines (**B**). Each will contain an image of a different god or goddess. The images are called **murtis**.

Hindus in the UK often gather for an **arti** service once a week. Worshippers take off their shoes on entering the temple. They bow before the deities and make an offering. Food offerings are blessed and later shared out among those present. There are no chairs. Everyone sits on the floor below the level of the deities. The worshippers sing devotional songs while the priest prepares the murtis. They are washed and dressed. Offerings of food, flowers and incense are placed before them. When the priest is ready, everyone stands for the offering of light.

A In India, a mandir is the house of a deity

18

3 *In the UK the mandir may have many shrines*

Worshippers may visit the temple even when there is no service. They perform puja, which involves making offerings at the shrine. They also pray, meditate or listen to readings from the scriptures. In the UK, the temple is often a community centre as well as a place of worship. Festivals and cultural events may be held there. Coffee mornings for senior citizens or mother and toddler groups are sometimes organized. Many temples run a youth club. Most young Hindus were born in the UK. They may have Gujurati or Punjabi as their mother tongue. The temple may offer language classes so that they can learn to read and write in their mother tongue.

Discussion question

Why do you think that Hindus in the UK like to gather together for worship?

Hindus believe that loving God should be expressed in showing love for other people. So friendship, hospitality and service to others are important. Volunteers work hard at the temple. They help provide transport for senior citizens, take language classes, clean, prepare food and raise money for charities.

THINGS TO DO

1 Imagine you are doing a TV programme on Hindu temples. You have one reporter in a mandir in India and one in a mandir in the UK. They are going to report back to you on different screens. Write a script for this three-way conversation which brings out the similarities and differences between the two mandirs.
2 Design a Hindu temple. Use your knowledge of Hinduism to help you decide how it should look, what it should contain and the symbols and images that you want to include. Write a paragraph to explain the design of your building.
3 Write a timetable of events for a poster covering a week of activities in a Hindu temple. Make sure it reflects the sense of community and the importance of language and culture. With a little research you should be able to fix a date for a festival!
4 Loving God should express itself in showing love to others. Why do you think that so many religious traditions see a connection between these two expressions of love? Write a poem, short play or story which explores this connection.

9 Who are the Jews?

One definition of a Jew is a person born to a Jewish mother. This suggests that there is a Jewish race or nation. The name 'Jew' is also given to people who follow the religion known as Judaism.

Traditionally, Jews are believed to be descended from the **prophet Abraham** and his grandson **Jacob**. Jacob became known as **Israel**. The photographs in this unit show that even if it were possible to prove such a beginning, today's Jews clearly belong to many races and nations (**A**, **B** and **C**).

The Jewish people settled in the land of Canaan, now known as Israel. However, wars and conflicts forced many to leave and live elsewhere. Over the years, Jewish communities developed in many countries. In some they lived quite separately and often they were not given the same rights as other people.

Discussion question

Although Jews were sometimes forced to live separately, some groups choose to keep themselves apart. Why do you think groups in school, or in society, choose to keep themselves separate?

A *These young Jews in Jerusalem originally came from Ethiopia*

B *An older generation Jew attending a synagogue in Kerala, India*

It was inevitable, however, that Jews mixed with non-Jews. Jewish presence made a difference in a country. In turn, Jewish culture and tradition were influenced by the societies in which Jews lived.

This situation has continued to the present day. In most countries Jews are now given the same rights as everyone else. They live and work alongside their non-Jewish neighbours. They are full citizens of the countries they live in. When they have to tell someone their nationality they describe themselves as, for example, British, French or American.

Intermarriage often takes place. Sometimes the non-Jewish partner becomes a Jew, or converts to Judaism. This involves learning about and accepting the history, teachings and practices of Judaism. Any children the couple have will be brought up as practising religious Jews.

Although the practice is not widespread, it is possible to become a Jew by choice, by choosing to follow the Jewish religion. Jews live in many countries of the world. The largest communities are to be found in the United States of America and in Israel.

C *An Ethiopian Jewish immigrant to Israel*

Some Jews, brought up as Jews themselves, choose not to keep the traditions and practices of Judaism. But this does not mean that they stop being Jewish. Any children they have may grow up learning and experiencing little, if anything, of Judaism. However, if their mother is Jewish, then so are they. They are part of the Jewish people. Some groups also regard children of Jewish fathers as Jewish.

THINGS TO DO

1 It is usually considered wise for marriage partners to have several things in common. They might share hobbies, interests, beliefs and values. They might come from similar backgrounds. What might be some of the difficulties which could arise when two people from different religious backgrounds choose to marry? What other differences in background could cause tensions in a marriage?

2 Jews have not always had equal rights with others in countries in which they have lived. Nowadays, in most places they do have full citizenship rights. Britain has a number of laws designed to make sure that everyone is treated fairly. However, laws alone cannot do away with prejudice and discrimination. How do laws and rules help to ensure equal rights for everyone? What else, besides laws, is needed to ensure equal rights for all?

3 Although many Jews see Israel as their spiritual home, it is not a country run on religious principles alone. There is some tension between strict religious Jews, who would like religious practices to be a stronger feature of life in their country, and secular, or non-religious, Jews, who do not want religion to be a strong influence on the way the country is run. Discuss the difficulties these tensions might cause.

4 At various times in history Jews have been forced to leave their homes and live elsewhere. People in many areas of the world today are forced into similar situations. Many have to become refugees. What are some of the difficulties and sadnesses they might face? How might a religious faith help in such situations?

10 The Tenakh

10

Jewish scriptures are known as the **Tenakh**. The word Tenakh comes from the Hebrew initial letters for **Torah**, Nevi'im and Ketuvim, the three sections of the Jewish Bible.

Ketuvim means 'writings'. This section contains several different sorts of books. For example, Ruth and Esther are read on festival occasions (**A**). Others, like Psalms, Proverbs and Ecclesiastes provide thoughts about God and his teachings as well as about life and how it should be lived.

> 'The Lord is merciful and good; our God is compassionate. The Lord protects the helpless.' (Psalm 116:5–6)

> 'Your teachings are wonderful; I obey them with all my heart. The explanation of your teachings gives light and brings wisdom to the ignorant.' (Psalm 119:129)

Discussion question

What impression of God is created by these verses from the Book of Psalms?

Nevi'im means 'prophets', the title given to someone who was believed to be a messenger of God. The prophets of Israel were people who spoke out against the corruption and injustice they saw in the society around them. They reminded their fellow Jews of how God wanted them to live.

The most important part of the Tenakh is the Torah. Torah means 'instruction' or 'teaching'. It contains five books, known as the Books of Moses. Tradition says God gave Moses both the written and the oral or spoken Torah. The written Torah contains God's instructions for living. The oral Torah explains and interprets these laws in order to help people understand them more fully. The oral Torah was originally passed on by word of mouth. It was eventually written down in a work called the **Mishnah**.

A *The story of Esther is read during the festival of Purim*

Rabbis, or teachers, have studied the Torah and Mishnah. Their thoughts and interpretations have been written down in the **Gemara**. The Mishnah and Gemara form a huge commentary on the Torah known as the **Talmud**. This helps Jews understand how God's instructions can be applied to their everyday lives.

The tradition of interpretation continues today. Medical science and technology make new things possible. Jews often ask rabbis for advice on these matters. Rabbis still study and debate the details of the Torah and Talmud so they can answer these questions (**B**).

Orthodox Judaism teaches that the Torah is the word of God exactly as it was revealed to Moses. It is as relevant today as it was then. All the instructions must be followed. **Reform Judaism** teaches that the Torah was written by a number of people who were inspired by God. They were also influenced by their own knowledge and the ideas of the times they lived in. The Reform tradition accepts that some parts of the Torah are not relevant to modern life so some instructions need not be followed.

B *Students still debate the Torah and Talmud*

THINGS TO DO

1 Choose one of the following verses from the Book of Proverbs and make a poster to illustrate its meaning.

'It is better to have a little, honestly earned, than to have a large income gained dishonestly.' (Proverbs 16:8)

'Kind words bring life, but cruel words crush your spirit.' (Proverbs 15:4)

'Correct someone, and afterwards he will appreciate it more than flattery.' (Proverbs 28:23)

2 One of the prophets, called Amos, criticized people for making a show of worshipping God while they did not put his instructions into practice in their daily lives. Both giving and receiving criticism can be difficult. Discuss reasons why this is so.

3 It has been traditional for those studying the Torah and Talmud to do so in pairs. What do you think might be the advantages of this?

4 The Talmud is important for understanding the meaning of the Torah. It is the work of very learned rabbis. In groups discuss what you think is meant by the following quotations, and what meaning and relevance they have today?

'Respect your father and your mother.' (Exodus 20:12)

What does it mean to respect your parents? How can young people show respect? What relevance has this to children who do not live with their parents?

'In such cases show no mercy; the punishment is to be a life for a life, an eye for an eye, a tooth for a tooth, a hand for a hand and a foot for a foot.' (Deuteronomy 19:21)

In what cases might this advice be appropriate? Do you think it should be taken literally? How else could it be interpreted?

The synagogue

The **synagogue** is the place where Jews meet, study and pray. In the Tenakh we can read about a time when the Jewish people had a settled life in Israel. They had a homeland and a temple in the city of Jerusalem. In the sixth century BCE many people were forced to leave Israel and to live in exile. They tried to meet in groups to hear the scriptures and worship together. Places where they met became known as synagogues, or 'meeting places'.

Every synagogue has a main hall where the congregation gathers for worship. Set in the wall facing Jerusalem, there is a large cupboard called the **Ark** or Aron Hakodesh. It contains the scrolls of the Torah which are usually behind an embroidered curtain.

Above the Ark there is often a quotation. Some have 'Know before whom you stand' written in Hebrew. This reminds Jews that God is present everywhere. There is often a representation of the two stone tablets on which Moses received the **Ten Sayings** or Ten Commandments. On the walls either side of the Ark there are often two prayers, one for the state of Israel and the other for the country the synagogue is in. In Britain this would be a prayer in English for the Queen and Royal Family. Most Jews look upon Israel as their spiritual homeland even if they have no desire to actually live there. The prophet Jeremiah told people God wanted them to play their part in the country in which they lived:

A *Inside an Orthodox synagogue*

Inside a Reform synagogue

'Work for the good of the cities where I have made you go ... Pray to me on their behalf, because if they are prosperous, you will be prosperous too.' (Jeremiah 29:7)

In front of the Ark is a small lamp called the **Ner Tamid** which is kept burning as a reminder of the eternal lamp of the temple in Jerusalem. Some say it symbolizes the belief that the light of the Torah will shine forever.

The reading of the Torah is an important part of synagogue services. This takes place on a raised platform called the **bimah**. Traditionally this is in the centre of the synagogue. However, in some Reform synagogues it is in front of the Ark.

In Orthodox synagogues men and women sit separately. Traditionally women sit in a gallery, which is sometimes screened. Services are led by men. In Reform synagogues men and women sit together and services may be led by men or women.

THINGS TO DO

1 Look at the photos in this unit. One is of an Orthodox synagogue (**A**) and the other a Reform synagogue (**B**). What clues can you find in each one to show which is which?

2 Some say the Ner Tamid symbolizes the idea that the light of the Torah will shine forever. Psalm 119:5 expresses a similar idea:

'Your word is a lamp to guide me and a light for my path.'

Explain this phrase in your own way. Create a symbol or illustration to represent the ideas behind it.

3 The prophet Jeremiah suggested that it was a duty to be involved in and work for the community in which you live. Discuss ways you could work for the good of:
   • your school
   • your local community.

4 Suggest some benefits of men and women worshipping:
   • separately
   • together.

The Torah

The word of God as it was said to have been revealed to Moses is written in Hebrew on a scroll called the **Sefer Torah**. It is handled with the greatest care and reverence. The manuscript itself is hand written by a **scribe** on parchment made from the skins of **kosher** animals. The work of a scribe is highly skilled (**A**). If he makes a mistake, the ink has to be removed from the parchment with a knife. If one of the names of God is written incorrectly, it cannot simply be erased. That section of the text has to be cut out and buried in a Jewish cemetery. It takes at least a year to write a whole scroll. Although it is hard work, it is also an act of love and worship.

B An open Ark displaying Torah scrolls

A A scribe writing a Torah scroll

The Sefer Torah is rolled on two wooden poles with handles. In most synagogues each scroll is wrapped in an embroidered mantle. Over this hangs a silver breastplate and a **yad**. This is a pointer made in the shape of a hand with an extended forefinger. It is used to help the reader follow the text. A silver crown, often with bells, is placed over the top of the two poles or one on each (**B**).

Dressing the Sefer Torah in this way is the tradition of the **Ashkenazim**. They are Jews who trace their ancestors through Eastern and Central European communities. The **Sephardim**, whose ancestors lived in Spain, put their scrolls in decorated wooden or metal cylinders (**C**).

C *A Sefer Torah in the Sephardim tradition*

Discussion question

Why do you think Jews choose to dress the Sefer Torah so elaborately?

During synagogue services, passages from the Torah are read. It is an honour for members of the congregation to open the Ark, to take out the scroll and carry it to the bimah. As it passes by, people lean forward to touch the mantle with the tassels of their **tallitot** and then they kiss them.

The Torah is divided into sections, one for each week so the whole scroll can be read in a year. It is read during services on Saturday, Monday and Thursday mornings. The reading of the Torah scroll never finishes though. As soon as the end is reached, the first passage is read again and so the cycle begins once more. The day on which the last and first portions are both read is a special one. It is called **Simchat Torah**, which means rejoicing over the Torah. There is a happy atmosphere in the synagogue. All the scrolls are taken out of the Ark and carried round the bimah. People sing and dance.

It is a great honour to be chosen to read the Torah on this day. The person called up for the last section is known as the bridegroom of the Torah. The one chosen for the first portion is the bridegroom of the beginning. Reform synagogues allow women to take these roles and so call them brides.

THINGS TO DO

1 Although Torah scrolls are very expensive, a synagogue needs to have more than one. Using the information in this unit, explain why this is so.
2 Write and illustrate a leaflet entitled, 'The importance of the Torah'. It should explain what it means to Jews and how they show this.
3 The Torah is read in Hebrew. What might be the advantages and difficulties of this for Jews in the various countries of the world?
4 Imagine you have been asked to make a short radio programme about Simchat Torah. This will include an interview with a Jewish person. What questions would you ask and why?

13 Prayer and worship

Jews can say their daily prayers and worship God anywhere. However, large synagogues, especially Orthodox ones, hold services every day because communal prayers are very important. The most well attended are on Friday evening and Saturday morning because many go to the synagogue on **Shabbat**. For worship to take place in Orthodox synagogues, there must be ten male Jews over the age of thirteen present (this is known as a **minyan**). In the Reform tradition the ten can be men or women. Some communities do not even insist on ten being present.

In services psalms and words of adoration are recited and prayers are said. The Sefer Torah, a symbol of God's love, is taken out of the Ark and a special blessing is said. The scroll is taken to the reading

B *A scroll being read at the bimah*

desk on the bimah (**A**). The decorations are removed. The scroll is then unwound and the text is chanted in Hebrew (**B**).

A *The Sefer Torah in a synagogue*

Each week several members of the congregation are called to the bimah for the reading. Anyone who is able to do so can read from the scroll. However, the Hebrew is written without vowels and the tune for each section has to be known by heart. Many find it difficult. So as not to embarrass poor readers, someone reads on behalf of those who are called up. Each person says the blessings at the beginning and end of their portion, however. The blessing recited after the reading is:

'Blessed are You, Lord our God, Ruler of the universe, who has given us a Torah of truth, so giving us eternal life. Blessed are You, Lord, Giver of Torah.'

Before the scroll is returned to the Ark it is held up high for everyone to see.

The **Shema** is said during morning and evening services. It is a statement of the Jewish belief that there is only one God. Prayers from the Talmud are recited. Prayers are also said for Israel and the country the synagogue is in. A prayer known as the **Aleinu** comes at the end of the service. It is about the greatness of God and his covenant with the Jewish people. It also looks forward to the coming of the **Messiah** when there will be peace in the world.

It is not necessarily a rabbi who takes the service. The hazzan or cantor who is able to chant the notes correctly leads the prayers. There are prayer books in Hebrew, with a translation for non-Hebrew speakers to follow the service (**C**). Many Reform synagogues have parts of the service in the language of the community. The atmosphere at the synagogue is friendly and relaxed. There is usually a hall and kitchen facilities available where people can meet socially after the service.

Discussion question

What do you think might be the benefits of having a social gathering after a religious service?

C A Hebrew prayer book with English translation

THINGS TO DO

1 Jewish men wear a head covering, such as the **kippah**, for prayer. They also wear the tallit. Time set aside for God is marked out by these visible signs. When we go out or meet someone important we may dress up. What does it show when we do this? What do you think it means when religious people wear special clothes for worship? Discuss these questions in class.

2 The Talmud suggests one should say 100 blessings a day. Make a list of all the things for which you could be grateful in the space of a day. Can you make it up to 100? Share your ideas.

3 Appointing someone to read from the Torah on behalf of those who find it difficult is not only an act of kindness to them. It is also a way of ensuring that the Torah is always read and heard correctly.
Why is this important?

4 For Jews the Torah is a symbol of God's love and faithfulness. Design your own symbol to represent God's love and faithfulness. Explain what the features of your symbol represent.

Shabbat in the home

Jews meet in synagogues to worship and study together. However, it is often said that the home is the centre of Jewish life and education. It is here that Judaism is taught and lived.

Jewish life revolves around Shabbat. Jews believe God told them to keep the seventh day of the week holy. Shabbat is a day of rest which should be separate and different from other days. In many homes it is a day for the family to be together. Everything has to be got ready because for 24 hours no work is done. Food has to be prepared in advance.

Just before the sun sets on Friday evening the mother of the household lights two candles to welcome the day. She says a blessing:

> 'Blessed are You O Lord our God, Ruler of the universe, Who has made us holy by Your commandments and has commanded us to light the Shabbat candles.'

Some people may go to the synagogue service before returning home for a special Friday night meal.

Discussion question

In the Jewish tradition, each day begins in the evening. This suggests that sleep is seen as a preparation for the day rather than something one falls into when the day is over. What do you think of this idea?

A *A Shabbat table*

he table is laid with the best cloth and ⋯ina (**A**). Before the meal the father blesses ⋯s children and sings a song from the Book ⋯ Proverbs in praise of his wife. Then he ⋯cites or sings **Kiddush**. This is the blessing ⋯er the wine. Even the children drink ⋯me. At this point members of the family ⋯ash their hands. The **challot** are then ⋯essed. These are two loaves of special ⋯ead for Shabbat. Everyone receives a piece ⋯ the first slice which is sprinkled with a ⋯ttle salt. This is a reminder of the salt ⋯rinkled on the sacrifices which were ⋯ade in the Temple in ancient times.

Shabbat is a time dedicated to God and some families read the Torah and share their thoughts on its teachings. Traditionally it has been a custom to invite a guest for Shabbat. It might be a friend or relative or a stranger who is far from their own home or family.

Shabbat ends when three faint stars can be seen in the sky on Saturday evening. At the close of Shabbat a prayer called **Havdalah** is said (**B**). The Havdalah separates Shabbat from the new week. When the Havdalah is said a long plaited or twisted candle is lit. At the same time a little box of sweet spices is lifted up and passed around the family for everyone to smell the last sweetness of Shabbat. The father takes a sip of sweet wine and Shabbat is drawn to a close. Everyone hopes that its sweetness will last through the week ahead.

THINGS TO DO

1   In what ways is Judaism learned by living it?
2   Using this and unit 13 write an article or create a poster to describe and explain how Jews celebrate Shabbat.
3   In the hustle and bustle of modern life, many families find it hard to spend much time together. What do you think might be some of the benefits and challenges of having a family day each week?
4   Jews believe God told them not to work on Shabbat, but it is not always easy to understand what is meant by work. Jews were told there were 39 activities, like sewing, building and lighting fires, that they must not do. Rabbis interpret the Jewish law and explain how these apply to modern life. For example, lighting a fire can include switching on an electric light. Many Reform Jews reject this way of looking at things. They interpret work to be what they do for a living. What do you understand by the idea of not working on Shabbat? How would putting this idea into practise change:
    • what you do
    • what members of your family do?

Havdalah is said at the close of Shabbat

Learning and living Judaism

Education is an important part of Jewish life. The word of God, recorded in the Tenakh, can only influence people if they understand what it says. For this reason many synagogues provide classes on Sundays, and sometimes in evenings, for young people to learn more about their religion. They are encouraged to study the scriptures and learn to read Hebrew (**A**).

Members of the Jewish community train to teach in these 'religion schools'. In some, classes are only provided for young people up to the age of 13. Others also take older children, and some offer GCSE courses in religious studies and/or Hebrew.

Discussion question

What would you be prepared to spend time studying outside school hours?

Some parents choose to send their children to Jewish schools if they are available (**B**). Here, lessons in Hebrew and Judaism are built into the timetable.

A *Children studying Hebrew*

A Jewish day school in London

Jews must learn the teachings of Judaism because each one has a personal responsibility to live by the instructions God has given. They believe God will judge them by how well they have done. This is not just a matter of knowing and keeping all the mitzvot or commandments. Many Jews believe they need to *feel* their loyalty to God and have a desire to do what he wants.

For some, for example Orthodox Jews, this will mean strictly keeping all the laws and applying them to the changing situations of life. For others, for example Reform Jews, this will mean reinterpreting some laws and giving up those they consider to be out of date. However, for all it will mean trying to develop the personal qualities which help them to show God's love for the whole world. This idea is expressed in Leviticus 19:17–18:

> *'Do not bear a grudge against anyone, but settle your differences with him … Do not take revenge on anyone or continue to hate him, but love your neighbour as you love yourself.'*

Jews believe God requires them to be truthful, honest and fair. Leviticus 19:35–6 gives an example of this:

> *'Do not cheat anyone by using false measures of length, weight, or quantity. Use honest scales, honest weights, and honest measures.'*

Courtesy and good manners are encouraged. The Book of Proverbs says:

> *'A gentle answer quietens anger, but a harsh one stirs it up.'* (15:1)

Many Jews believe God will judge them not so much on how accurately they have followed his instructions but rather on their intentions. For example, the motives people have for giving gifts can be very different. A famous Jewish teacher called Moses Miamonides identified different kinds of givers, including those who give when asked, those who give without being asked, and those who give without the receiver knowing. Those who give generously and without thought of personal reward live the way Jews believe God wants.

THINGS TO DO

1 Many people would agree that it is good to be truthful, honest and fair. Why is it sometimes difficult to live up to these ideals? Give examples.

2 Giving gentle answers in angry situations can call for great patience. Write a story to illustrate how patience can help in difficult circumstances.

3 Discuss why education and learning are important for Jews. Think about your education so far. What have you valued most about it? Discuss your thoughts in class.

4 What do you think about the personal qualities mentioned in this unit? What kind of personal qualities would you like to develop? Explain why.

The Buddha's enlightenment

Buddhism started in India and soon spread. As it did so, it grew in different ways. It is a rich and varied religious tradition and its followers can be found in many countries of the world.

All forms of Buddhism have grown from the experience and teachings of one man called Gotama Buddha. The word **Buddha** means 'Enlightened Being'. Buddhists believe there have been and will be other Buddhas.

When Gotama gained **enlightenment** it was as if he had woken from a dream. He realized that up until then he had not understood the truth about life. His understanding was no longer clouded. He could see clearly. He was filled with compassion for people who were struggling through life, with its many difficulties and times of unhappiness. He decided to devote the rest of his life to helping others and teaching them the way to **Nibbana** (**A**).

Discussion question

Think of times when you have come to understand something clearly for the first time. How did this make you feel?

The Buddha first told others what he had learned about life in a place called Benares in India. These teachings became known as the **Four Noble Truths**.

- He explained that life is unsatisfactory. Everyone experiences discontent, unhappiness and suffering.
- He said he had discovered the reasons why life is like this. People are always wanting things. He said this attitude was due to greed, hatred and ignorance. No matter what they have, people always seem to want more or something different. Even when they have what they want, they worry about losing it. People are like this because they do not understand that it is their own minds which are creating the problems. They are often filled with a sense of their importance. They want to make their own lives better and to have things which they think will make them happy. The Buddha said this was not possible because everything changes – including people and what they want – and

A *A Buddha rupa depicting the Buddha teaching*

B *The lotus flower in bloom*

nothing lasts forever. The Buddha knew that people find it hard to accept that their own lives will not go on forever.

The way to stop suffering and discontent is to stop wanting. This is very hard. However, the Buddha said he had found a way.

The way to stop wanting is to follow the **Eightfold Path** (see unit 17).

THINGS TO DO

1 The idea of enlightenment in Buddhism is not easy to explain. The lotus (**B**) is often used as a symbol to illustrate it. It grows in deep muddy water (people's ignorance leads to a discontented life) and becomes a beautiful flower (by following the right path people can gain enlightenment). This unit has also described gaining enlightenment as being like waking from a dream. What other descriptions or illustrations could you use?

2 The Buddha told others he had discovered something important about life. He said that life is unsatisfactory, that everyone experiences discontent, unhappiness and suffering. This is because people want things they cannot have or try to hold on to things and people that will inevitably change and die. Although this was his understanding, he always encouraged his followers to think for themselves and to test out what he said to see if it seemed true. Do you agree with his description of life? Explain your reasons.

3 According to the Buddha, all discontent is due to wanting. Do you agree? What part do greed, hatred and ignorance play? Think of three examples of discontent or unhappiness. In pairs, discuss the causes behind each example.

4 In the Buddhist wheel of eternal rebirth (**C**), greed, hatred and ignorance are symbolized by a cockerel, snake and pig respectively. Discuss why each of these was chosen. Devise your own symbols for these three characteristics.

The Buddhist wheel of eternal rebirth

The Dhamma

The Buddha's teachings are called the **Dhamma**. He gave his followers advice on how to live their lives so they could put an end to feelings of discontent and find peace. These guidelines are called the Eightfold Path, which sets out a middle way. The Buddha said people should not live life in luxury because this distracts them from the spiritual path. Nor should they live in great hardship because people who do are only able to concentrate on surviving.

The eight aspects to this path are not steps to be followed one after another. They all work together to help people towards Nibbana. The first aspect, however, is very important in pointing people in the right direction.

- Right understanding – This means waking up to the truth about the way things are.

The Buddha taught that people need to understand that nothing remains unchanged nor lasts forever. Even the universe, which will go on for a very long time, will not last forever. People like the security of things and people they know but they cannot always have them. Relationships change and people die. This belief that nothing is permanent is called **anicca**. The Buddha said that when we cling to things to stay the same we only make ourselves and others unhappy.

- Right thought – A person can be harmed by their thoughts. Thoughts of greed, hatred, envy and unkindness make a person feel unhappy with their life as it is
- Right speech, Right action and Right livelihood – These are possible when negative thoughts are stopped. People should try to put selfishness behind them and live without doing any harm to others. This means trying to be truthful and helpful in what is said, and avoiding gossip. People should try to be kind to all

A *The flower in bud*

The flower in full blossom

C *The blossom withers and dies*

living beings. For many Buddhists this means they will not eat meat. The Buddha taught that people should earn their living without taking advantage of others.
Right effort – People must work constantly to overcome greed, hatred and ignorance.
Right mindfulness or awareness – This means being very clear about one's intentions in life. It also means accepting that everything changes. People who are able to do so might not feel so angry, frustrated and hurt by things that happen.

Discussion question

Think back over the last week. Discuss how Buddhist teachings might have helped you, or someone you know, deal with unwanted change.

Right concentration – This is achieved through meditation (see unit 22) and self-discipline.
hen the Buddha had explained these
eas to his followers he said:

'Go now and wander out of compassion for the world, for the benefit, welfare and happiness of gods and men. Teach the Dhamma.'

THINGS TO DO

1 The photos (**A**, **B** and **C**) in this unit show how a flower changes and dies. Design your own symbol or illustration to represent the idea that everything changes.
2 Make three sets of two columns with the headings:
   • Right speech – wrong speech
   • Right action – wrong action
   • Right livelihood – wrong livelihood.
   Think about these aspects of the Eightfold Path and their opposites. Write examples under each heading.
3 The Buddha said people should live a life of moderation, avoiding extremes. In what ways do you think a life of luxury might distract people from spiritual aspects of life? Why might a person living a life of great hardship find it difficult to concentrate on spiritual things?
4 The Buddha taught that a person's intentions are very important. Discuss examples of how unacceptable things can happen even when people have good intentions and how good things can happen even when people have bad intentions. Do you think intentions are important? Explain your answer.

18 The Sangha

The first disciples of the Buddha followed his example. They gave up the usual pattern of work, home and family to become wandering monks, meditating and teaching the Dhamma. This was how Buddhism first began. The Buddha's following grew and spread. Many Buddhists today still devote their lives to the quest for Nibbana. Many still choose to join communities of monks and nuns.

Monks and nuns of the **Theravada** tradition are known as **bhikkhus** and **bhikkhunis**. This means 'those who receive **alms**' because they rely on the local community for gifts of food and provisions. The community of monks and nuns is called the **Sangha**. In some places the word is used to mean all members of the Buddhist community.

Members of the Theravada Sangha begin their day before dawn with meditation and religious chants. In Buddhist countries, after a simple breakfast, they go into the community with their alms bowls to collect food for the day (**A**). The main meal of the day is eaten by noon. After this, nothing else is eaten. Time is spent studying the teaching of the Buddha, practising meditation (**B**), offering devotion at the shrine of the Buddha and listening to talks given by senior monks. **Lay** Buddhists consider it a privilege to support monks and nuns. Westernized Buddhist groups, however, do not rely on gifts from lay Buddhists. Members often work during the day, running businesses so the Sangha can be self-supporting.

The Buddha's example and teachings are very important as is the support of others in the community. Members of the Sangha remind themselves of this when they say regularly the **Three Jewels**:

A Buddhist monks on their alms round in Bangkok, Thailand

Buddhist nuns in meditation

'I take refuge in the Buddha, I take refuge
the Dhamma and I take refuge in the
ngha.'

All Buddhists try to keep Five Precepts.
hey should:

1 Refrain from killing or injuring living
creatures
2 Refrain from taking what is not given
3 Refrain from any sexual misconduct
4 Refrain from lying and wrong speech
5 Refrain from taking alcohol or misusing
drugs

hen they enter the Sangha, monks and
ins keep a further five. They should also:

6 Refrain from eating after midday
7 Refrain from taking part in entertainments,
such as music and dancing
8 Avoid using jewellery and perfumes
9 Refrain from sleeping in a luxury bed
10 Refrain from handling money.

Discussion question

*What do you think you would miss most if you
were living the life of a Buddhist monk? What
might you gain by living a life like this?*

lly ordained Theravada monks have
most no possessions. The only things they
ve are a bowl, their robes and a razor for
aving. Monks and nuns shave all the hair

on their heads as a sign of living simply and
giving up self-pride. Members of
westernized Buddhist groups do not
necessarily wear robes or shave their heads.

THINGS TO DO

1 Monks and nuns have very few possessions.
Those they have symbolize the kind of life
they live. Write a short article about the
things they have and their significance.

2 What do you think is meant by the words, 'I
take refuge in…'? What things do people
normally take refuge in in our society?
Design a poster to show your ideas.

3 Lay Buddhists as well as monks and nuns try
to keep the first Five Precepts. Each one
gives advice on what people should not do.
Write a positive version of each precept. In
other words, what is the opposite which
people should aim for?

4 The practices of Theravada monks and nuns
developed in countries with a strong
Buddhist tradition. Theravada monks and
nuns are noticeable in Britain because they
wear robes and shave their heads. Members
of westernized Sangha choose not to stand
out in this way. Discuss what you think are
the advantages of both approaches to
Buddhism in Britain.

19 Buddhist scriptures

Dhamma is a very important word for Buddhists. It can be translated in many ways. It could be said to mean 'the truth about the way things are'. It can be interpreted as 'law' or 'what is right'. It can also be translated as 'teaching' or the 'Word of the Buddha'. Dhamma is contained in the teaching of the Buddha. For Buddhists it is the Truth. However, the Buddha said no one should just accept his teaching. Each person must test it for themselves in their own experience.

The teaching of the Buddha was treasured by his first followers. After his death they recited his teachings and memorized them. The words were handed down in different dialects and languages. The most complete collection of these teachings is in the language of Pali. The **Pali Canon** is the name given to the scriptures of the Theravada tradition. They are called the **Tipitaka** or 'the three baskets'. The Tipitaka contains the sayings of the Buddha, his rules of discipline for bhikkhus, and philosophical discussion on the teachings.

Mahayana Buddhists have their own texts in Sanskrit, Chinese, Tibetan and Japanese as well as Pali. They make up a treasure house of stories, teachings and ideas to help people on the path to enlightenment. Many of the texts are the same as those of the Tipitaka. Some may be later teachings which have been handed down with the Buddha's own words.

Most Buddhist Sangha have a library containing copies of the scriptures so that

A *Buddhist monks studying the scriptures*

B *Buddhist scriptures written on palm leaves*

people can study them (**A**). Sometimes the scriptures are displayed in the shrine or meditation room. They are given a place of honour because they contain the word of the Buddha. Some are copies which have been hand-written on palm leaves (**B**).

The Buddha knew that people needed to be taught in a variety of ways to help them to understand as fully as possible. He was quite happy for the Dhamma to be translated. Sometimes he used stories to help people remember and understand his teachings.

Discussion question

Stories have been used by many great teachers. Why do you think this is so?

The story of Kisa Gotami shows how Dhamma can be found in experience as well as teachings.

Kisa Gotami was the mother of a young boy. Her son became ill and died. She was beside herself with grief. Picking up the boy, she went from house to house asking for medicine, but of course no one could help her. Then she met a wise man who suggested she ask the Buddha. The Buddha said he could help her. He sent her to collect three grains of mustard seed, each one from a house in which no one had ever died. As Kisa Gotami went from home to home she found out that every household had lost a loved one. Everyone had a sadness in their life. Humbled by what she had learnt, she cremated her son and returned to the Buddha to follow his teaching.

THINGS TO DO

1 Imagine there is to be an exhibition in your local library of different kinds of books. One of the books on display will be Buddhist scriptures written on palm leaves. Each exhibit needs a card nearby to provide information about it. Write the card to go with the Buddhist scriptures.

2 Kisa Gotami's experience helped her to understand that death comes to everyone; nothing remains unchanged. Write about an experience you or someone else has had from which a worthwhile lesson was learnt.

3 For a long while the Buddha's teachings were taught from memory by teachers. Later they were written down. What do you think are the advantages of learning by:
 • listening to a teacher
 • reading written ideas and information?

4 The Buddha taught people what he had come to understand about life. However, he encouraged them to test out his teachings in their own lives. He wanted people to think for themselves, not just to accept his ideas without question. How important is it for people to think for themselves? Do you think it is easy? Explain your answers.

Supporting one another

The Buddha taught that everything is dependent on other things. What a person does has effects on other parts of their life and on the lives of others. Buddhists believe in **rebirth**. The Buddha said that there is no such thing as the 'self' which remains unchanged and passes from life to life until it reaches Nibbana. This idea is called anatta. People are made up of characteristics like feelings, thoughts and beliefs, which change all the time. These will continue to exist in a new life but will be combined in different ways.

What the next life will be like depends on what people have chosen to do in this one. Actions that affect life are called a person's **kamma**. This is a sort of unwritten record of what a person has done. Good kamma leads to improvements in this life and the next. Bad kamma makes situations worse. This is often called the law of cause and effect. The Buddha taught that a person's kamma depends on what they intended to do. Things that happen by accident do not count.

Buddhists believe it is important to work towards Nibbana for themselves and also to help others. The Buddha taught that people should show loving kindness (**metta**) to all living beings. These ideas are shown clearly in the ways in which the monastic and lay communities rely on each other and help one another. In the Theravada tradition, lay Buddhists provide food and money for monks and nuns. They believe this earns them **merit** (spiritual reward). The monks and nuns provide teaching and spiritual guidance to help others towards Nibbana.

This relationship is an important part of Buddhism even in countries, like Britain, where Buddhists are relatively few in number. Instead of the monks and nuns going out to the lay community to receive alms, Buddhists can visit monasteries and take food to the Sangha. In this case they might go into the room in which the monks and nuns will eat, where a place will be set out for each member of the community. The monks and nuns receive the food which is offered in silence (**A**). Giving alms is an act of loving kindness. It is believed to bring blessing to those who give as well as those who receive. Before eating, the Sangha recites a traditional blessing. Those who brought the food listen quietly and thoughtfully.

Discussion question

Followers of many religions say blessings or give thanks for food before they eat it. Why do you think they do this? Can others learn anything from this practice?

A *Monks and nuns receiving food in a temple*

B *People listening to a Buddhist teacher in a London temple*

Buddhist centres belonging to all the major branches of Buddhism (Theravada, Mahayana and **Vajrayana**) welcome visitors. Members of the Sangha often give talks about the Buddha and his teachings. People go to learn more about Buddhism and seek advice from the Sangha (**B**). Lessons are also given in meditation (see unit 22). Some communities also offer classes for children.

The Sangha is an inspiring symbol in the community. Members have given up a materialistic way of life for a spirtual way of life. They show how people can live happily without wealth and possessions. They also give advice on how to make right decisions and choices based on correct motivation.

THINGS TO DO

1 The Buddha said that everything we do has effects elsewhere. Do you agree? Is there anything you do which does not affect anyone or anything else? How much of your life is affected by what others do? Discuss your ideas in class.

2 Write briefly about ways in which the lay and monastic communities support one another.

3 The Buddha taught that a person builds up a record of the things they have done intentionally. This is called kamma. The things we do and say leave an impression on other people even after we have gone. When you leave school, how would you like your teachers and fellow students to remember you? Do you think this is the impression you have created so far? Explain your answers.

4 When the first Buddhist communities were set up in Britain some people were suspicious, some were tolerant, others were welcoming. Imagine a Buddhist Sangha is to be set up in your neighbourhood. Write a selection of letters to the editor of the local newspaper. Some letters should express the hopes and concerns of people in the neighbourhood. Others should explain the hopes of the Buddhist community. You could use a computer to set this out like the letters page of a newspaper.

21 The shrine

Many Buddhists have a Buddha **rupa**, or image, on a high shelf in their homes. It reminds them of the Buddha and the inspiration of his example and teaching. It is often used as the focus for meditation. Devotional offerings are also made. These are usually of incense, light and flowers.

Discussion question

Why do you think the Buddha rupa is usually placed on a high shelf?

It is not necessary for Buddhists to meet together to meditate or to give devotional gifts. However, many do choose to visit shrines and join with others. Shrines are always beautiful. This is considered to be important. Many contain a Buddha rupa and as people enter they will often put their hands together to bow to it. They might stand in front of it and touch their forehead, mouth and chest with their hands together. The body, speech and mind are all involved in offering devotion. (Buddhists believe the mind, which is not the same as the brain, is situated where the heart is.)

A *In Mahayana shrines there might be images of buddhas and bodhisattvas other than Gotama Buddha*

B *Prayer wheels are common in Tibet*

People sit quietly contemplating the image or meditating. Some find it helpful to repeat the words of a mantra. This is like a simple prayer or blessing. A **mala**, or string of prayer beads, may be used to keep count of the times the mantra is repeated. Monks, or priests, make the offerings and chant scriptures and devotional words like these:

> *'In reverence to the Buddha we offer incense*
> *Incense whose fragrance fills the air*
> *The fragrance of the perfect life, sweeter than incense*
> *Spreads in all directions throughout the world.'*

The image seen in Theravada shrines is of Gotama Buddha. In Mahayana shrines it might be the Buddha or any other buddha or **bodhisattva** (A). It is believed that there are many buddhas. Although they rarely appear n earth they live in other realms of the niverse. A Bodhisattva is a being who puts ff entry into Nibbana in order to work in ie world to help others.

Tibetan centres often have **thankas** to elp meditation. These are paintings of uddhas, religious symbols and symbolic cenes. The Buddhist wheel of eternal ebirth on page 35 is an example of a hanka. There may also be prayer flags and vheels (**B**), on which a mantra is written. urning the wheel is like saying the mantra.

Zen Buddhist centres sometimes have ardens. These are quite often made of rocks et in sand. The sand is raked into a simple attern (**C**). People use these to help their neditation. Beautiful gardens are often ound at other Buddhist centres. They help o create harmony and a peaceful tmosphere. They also remind Buddhists of he cycle of life, that nothing remains nchanged forever.

THINGS TO DO

1 Buddhists often touch their foreheads, mouths and chests when offering devotion to the Buddha. Explain how the body, speech and mind are each involved in offering devotion.
2 Read again the devotional words about the offering of incense. Explain what you think they mean.
3 Produce an information leaflet, with illustrations, entitled, 'Buddhist shrines and places of meditation'.
4 Turning prayer wheels in the Tibetan tradition is like saying the mantra written on them. It is as if the words are being released into the world to have some positive influence. Many people believe words are very powerful. In what ways might this be true? Do you believe thoughts have power? What do you think might be meant by 'the power of positive thought'? Discuss your ideas in class.

C A Zen Buddhist sand and rock garden

22 Meditation

Learning to meditate is an important part of what it is to be a Buddhist. Two aspects of the Eightfold Path (see page 36) are 'right mindfulness' and 'right concentration'. The Buddha said that these could be achieved through meditation, training the mind to be calm, not distracted or out of control.

The Buddha gave his followers guidance on several types of meditation to help with this. One form focuses on the person's breathing. For this the Buddha recommended that people sit cross-legged with a straight back. Sitting up straight, but not stiffly, is more important than being cross-legged so it is possible to do this seated in a chair (**A**). In this position Buddhists concentrate on their breathing. They do not

B *Japanese Zen Buddhist tea ceremony*

try to change it but just become aware of it. At first this is difficult because a person's thoughts jump from one thing to another. After much practice it is possible to be aware only of breathing and to hear nothing else. Many Buddhists say that if they are able to do this for short periods during the day it makes them feel refreshed and rested.

Discussion question

Why do you think sitting upright is important for this form of meditation? Why is it important not to be stiff or tense?

Other forms of meditation encourage people to become intensely observant, aware and mindful of anything and everything they do. This form of meditation can be done anywhere and anytime. It encourages people to become very aware of the present moment and experience the pleasure of it, rather than thinking of the past or planning for or worrying about the future.

In this form of meditation it is important for a person to concentrate on whatever it is they are doing rather than on themselves doing it. Forms of Japanese Zen Buddhism,

A *It is possible to meditate while seated in a chair*

Japanese flower arranging (ikebana)

or example, use a tea ceremony as a way of meditating (**B**). Those who do this must focus on the tea and how it is prepared rather than on what *they* are doing with it. Flower arranging (ikebana) (**C**), archery and walking are other activities which Zen Buddhists use as ways of meditating.

Another form of meditation concentrates on feelings as a way of overcoming negative emotions like anger and envy. Buddhists are encouraged to become aware of the feelings they have and look at them as if from the outside so that such emotions do not gain control. They observe what started the feelings, the effect they are having and how they die away. This is not a matter of judging good and bad feelings. It is about being aware of what is really happening.

Buddhists believe that meditation helps them towards Nibbana. The Buddha taught:

'The one who protects his mind from greed, anger and foolishness, is the one who enjoys real and lasting peace.'

THINGS TO DO

1 If you were able to interview a Buddhist about their meditation practice, what questions would you ask and why?
2 Write an article for a magazine entitled 'Buddhist meditation'. Include information about several kinds of meditation and their benefits. (You may also find unit 21 helpful.)
3 Do you agree with the Buddha's suggestion that we tend to ignore the present because we are often thinking of either the past or the future? Try to give examples to back up your view. Discuss this in class.
4 Try to still your mind with a breathing meditation. Try sitting up straight without being tense. Place your hands comfortably in your lap. You might like to close your eyes. Try to concentrate on your breathing. As other thoughts come into your mind don't fight them, just let them pass away as if they were separate. Focus on your breathing again. Afterwards discuss how you felt.

23

Christian belief in God: Three in one

Christians believe in one God. For them he is so great it is not possible for human beings to understand him fully. However, they believe it is possible to know God as a personal friend.

A Christian way of trying to understand God is to speak of him as three in one. God is understood to be Father, Son and Holy Spirit (**A**). This belief is called the Trinity. Father, Son and Holy Spirit are not three separate beings but different ways of being God. They are different ways of God making himself known to people (**B**).

From the early centuries of Christianity followers thought it was important to be able to say what the shared beliefs of Christians were. **Creeds** were drawn up to make these clear. The **Nicene Creed** is still used in many churches. It sets out beliefs about the Trinity as shown in this extract:

'We believe in one God,
the Father, the almighty,
maker of heaven and earth,
of all that is,
seen and unseen.
We believe in one Lord, Jesus Christ,
the only Son of God,
eternally begotten of the Father,
God from God, Light from Light,
true God from true God,
begotten, not made,
of one Being with the Father...
...We believe in the Holy Spirit,
the lord, the giver of life,
who proceeds from the Father and
the Son.
With the Father and the Son he is
worshipped and glorified...'

Discussion question

What do you think were (and still are) the advantages and difficulties for Christians of having a statement of shared beliefs?

As the Father, God is believed to be creator of all things. This does not mean that all Christians believe he made the world in six days, as described in the beginning of the book of Genesis in the Bible. Many believe the story illustrates the creative power of God rather than being literally true.

God is believed to have no beginning and no end. Christians believe he is present in the world and cares about people. He has given them guidelines for life. Although people fall short of the ideals he wants them to live up to, God will forgive those who are sorry.

God the Son is the second person of the Trinity. Christians believe that because he loved the world, God showed himself in the person of Jesus. Many believe Jesus was

A *Christians believe God is three in one*

Many symbols have been devised to represent the Trinity such as the Triangular Lodge in Rushton, Northamptonshire

terally the Son of God, that God was the ther of Jesus in a miraculous way. Others lieve the stories show Jesus was a very pecial person. Some say he was a man led with the spirit and goodness of God. e was in some way God and man together. e was both human and divine.

The Holy Spirit completes the Trinity. The pirit is seen as God's presence in people d in the world. He is believed to bring mfort and inspiration to individual lievers and the Christian community.

THINGS TO DO

1 Look at the photos in this unit. What impressions do they create of the Trinity?

Do you find them helpful or not? Discuss your answers in a group and give reasons for your views.

2 Design a symbol, picture or collage to illustrate the Christian idea of the Trinity.

3 Read the extract from Nicene Creed. Make a list in your own words of what it claims Christians believe about the Trinity. Form a group and compare your notes with those of others. Discuss the parts you found difficult to understand and see if you can work out what they might mean.

4 Coming to a statement of agreed beliefs is not always easy. Work in a group to see if you can draw up a short list of beliefs about life upon which you are all agreed. Could the whole class agree a list?

24 The Bible

One of the ways Christians learn about their religion, its teachings and beliefs, is by reading the **Bible** (**A**). The Bible is a collection of books which make up the scriptures of Christianity. There are two main sections. The larger contains writings from Jewish scriptures. As the first Christians were Jewish their scriptures were the Torah and Tenakh (see unit 10). These were written in Hebrew. They became part of the Christian Bible, known as the **Old Testament**.

The other section, called the **New Testament**, contains writings by Christians. Most were originally written in Greek (**B**).

B *The New Testament was originally written in Greek*

A *Christians learn about their religion through the Bible*

Many would say the most important of these are the **Gospels**. These were written inspire faith in Jesus Christ. They tell of hi life and teachings. Also in the New Testament are letters from St Paul and othe church leaders who were writing to the firs Christian communities. These contain words of guidance and encouragement for members of the Church. Another book called the Acts of the Apostles, which preaches the message and story of the early Christian Church.

In the early centuries of Christianity other writings were also shared. Some Christians thought they did not all teach th true message of the Christian faith. Meetin were held to discuss which should be included in the Bible. Final agreement was reached in the fourth century CE. The writings included are known as the **canon** of scripture.

The Bible is very important for Christians. They read it to discover what God taught through the prophets of the Old Testament and to learn about the life and teachings of Jesus and his early followers i the New Testament.

Discussion question

In what ways do you think the Bible is helpful t Christians?

The loaves and fishes

A large crowd had followed Jesus and his disciples to Bethsaida. When evening came the disciples suggested Jesus should send the people away so they could get something to eat. Jesus said 'You yourselves give them something to eat'. They answered 'All we have are five loaves and two fish.

Do you want us to go and buy food for this whole crowd?' There were about 5000 people there. Jesus told his disciples to get the people to sit in groups of fifty. He thanked God for the loaves and fish, broke them and gave them to the disciples to give out. Everyone ate and had enough.

(Mark 6:30–44)

ome Christians believe the Bible *is* the ord of God. They claim the words in the ble came directly from God and were ritten down exactly as they were given. any more, however, believe the Bible *ontains* the Word of God and that the riters were inspired by God. They wrote in eir own words and also used the ideas and nderstandings of the times in which they ved. Many parts of the Bible are believed to ach important messages and truths. But any say that not everything is meant to ply for all time. Readers with this view ill concentrate mainly on understanding e message without worrying too much out the detail of what is written.

THINGS TO DO

1 The Bible is a very important book for Christians. It helps them to understand life and how they should live. Think of some books you have found helpful. How was the help they provided similar to or different from the help Christians find in the Bible?

2 The canon of scripture was agreed upon to ensure that the Bible contained writings which taught the Christian message correctly. Each day newspapers report the issues of our time, often giving slightly different versions of the same stories. What are the advantages and disadvantages of reading only one newspaper's version of events? Is it important that we try to get the most accurate information?

3 The books of the Bible were not originally written in English. There are several English translations of the Bible which have been made at different times. Translations can be inaccurate. One story found in the Old Testament tells of how Moses led the Hebrew slaves out of Egypt to a new life in the desert. English translations have told they escaped miraculously through the Red Sea. This is a huge expanse of sea. It would have been a most spectacular event. Some scholars say the Hebrew words have not been correctly translated. It should be the Sea of Reeds, a marshy area. This would not necessarily mean a miracle was not needed. However, it does change the feel of the story. In what sense might possible inaccuracies in English translations of the Bible give Christians problems? How could these difficulties be overcome?

4 Read the story of the loaves and fish in the box on this page. Some say that Jesus multiplied the bread and fishes. Others say it is a story about sharing. In groups discuss what you think the message might be.

25 Jesus

Christians believe that God showed himself in the world in the life of Jesus. They read the Gospels in the New Testament to find out about him. He is shown as a challenging teacher, a healer and a friend to people from all walks of life.

Jesus showed the love of God in his care for others. There are many stories of him healing the sick. One was about the blind man called Bartimaeus. He called to Jesus as he walked along the road. People told him to be quiet but he continued. Jesus asked him what he wanted. Bartimaeus told him he wanted to see again. Jesus said:

'Go, your faith has made you well.'
(Mark 10:52)

At once Bartimaeus was able to see (**A**).

Jesus was also concerned about people who were unpopular. Zacchaeus, for example, was a tax collector in Jericho. When Jesus was in the city, Zacchaeus climbed a tree so he would be able to see him (**B**). When Jesus saw him he told him to get down because he was going to stay in his house. People criticized Jesus for befriending such a man. He said he had come to save the lost.

A *Jesus healed blind Bartimaeus*

B *People criticized Jesus for befriending the tax collector Zacchaeus*

Luke's Gospel describes how Zacchaeus changed as a result of his meeting with Jesus. He gave money to the poor and repaid those he had cheated and gave them compensation.

Discussion question

Who are the unpopular people, the social outcasts, of our time and society?

The lives of both Bartimaeus and Zacchaeus were changed by their meeting with Jesus. Christians today believe that Jesus can still change lives. When people read about him and his message in the Bible they may be inspired and decide to follow the Christian way. Those who do become Christians try to practise what Jesus taught. In this way they can show the presence of God in the world today.

In a very famous part of Matthew's Gospel known as the Sermon on the Mount, Jesus said:

'Do not judge others… for God will judge you in the same way as you judge others.' (Matthew 7:1–2)

he garden tomb in Israel, said by some to be where Jesus' body was laid and where he came back to life

When asked what the greatest nmandment was, Jesus said there were o important ones:

'Love the Lord your God with all your heart, with all your soul, and with all your mind.' (Matthew 22:37)

'Love your neighbour as you love yourself.' (Matthew 22:39)

Those who put these teachings into ictice can change the lives of people they et just as Jesus did.

Christians believe it is not only their esent lives that are changed by Jesus. They lieve he came back to life after his enemies d crucified him (**C**). In doing this he >wed there is life after death. Christians lieve they will live a spiritual life with God 1en their earthly lives end.

THINGS TO DO

1 When Jesus told people not to judge others he went on to say:
'Why, then, do you look at the speck in your brother's eye, and pay no attention to the log in your own eye?... First take the log out of your own eye, and then you will be able to see clearly to take the speck out of your brother's eye.' (Matthew 7:3–5)
Discuss what this advice about not judging others might mean in practice. What might be the benefits and difficulties of using this advice as
- individuals
- groups?
Write a short story on the theme of judging, or not judging, others.

2 The ideal Christian life is sometimes described as the **Kingdom of God**. Some people think this refers to the new life a Christian has after the end of their earthly life. Others believe they can be part of the Kingdom of God during this life. Discuss with a partner what this might mean.

3 Jesus said, 'Love your neighbour as you love yourself.' What do you think he meant about
- loving ourselves
- loving our neighbours as we love ourselves?
Write up or illustrate your thoughts.

4 Unit 24 considers different ways in which Christians interpret and understand what they read in the Bible. Look again at the story of Bartimaeus in this unit. Discuss how Christians might differ in their interpretation of it. How might someone who understands it simply as a story to teach an important truth see it differently from someone who believes it is literally true?

The Church

After Jesus left the earth and went to heaven, his followers continued to spread his teaching. For a while people believed that those who had known Jesus best would have the most reliable versions of his message. As the early followers grew old and died, Christians had to learn from the books which had been gathered to form the New Testament.

The religion spread further afield and many who became Christians were unable to read. Others could not read the Bible because it was in languages they did not understand (see unit 24). They had to rely on experts to translate and explain what it meant. Gradually people were specially trained to understand the scriptures and to lead worship in ways which were believed to be correct. These became the leaders of the Church. Ordinary Christians, known as the **laity**, looked to the church leaders to teach them about their religion.

The Christian Church grew and developed in various ways. Different church groups formed into **denominations**, each expressing their Christian faith in a variety of ways. The denomination with the largest number of members is the **Roman Catholic Church**.

Roman Catholics believe St Peter, one of Jesus' **disciples**, was the first Bishop of Rome. This is another name for the head of the Roman Catholic Church who is also called the **Pope** (A). They believe Jesus told Peter he was the foundation of the Church and that the true beliefs of Christianity have been passed on from pope to pope through the centuries. In this position of power and importance the Pope can decide on new teachings of the Roman Catholic Church on his own. However, he has many **cardinals**, **bishops** and **priests** with whom he can consult.

Some other denominations, such as the **Orthodox Churches** and the **Church of**

A Pope John Paul II, the head of the Roman Catholic Chur

England, also have bishops and priests or **vicars** (**B**). Decisions are made by consultation amongst themselves. Leaders in other denominations are called **ministe** or **elders**.

All of these leaders have studied the Bi and the teachings of their Church in detail They have been trained to lead worship. It their job to guide congregations in their understanding of the Christian faith.

Discussion question

*Some groups do not have leaders. Members the **Society of Friends**, for example, worshi in silence and anyone may speak if they feel inspired to do so. What do you consider migl be the benefits and challenges of this?*

In the early years of the twentieth century there was a strong move to bring the different churches together. The movemer

Church leaders in a procession

came known as the **Ecumenical
Movement**. The Greek word *oikoumene*
means 'one world'. From the work of this
Movement the World Council of Churches
as set up in 1948. Over 300 churches have
become members. They recognize that
though there are differences between them
ey are all part of the Church of Christ.

The symbol of the World Council of Churches

THINGS TO DO

1 Look at the photos of church leaders (**A** and
B). They often stand out because of the
clothes they wear. What are the advantages
and disadvantages of this for them and
members of their congregations? (You might
like to find out more about what leaders of
various denominations wear and why.)

2 What do you think are the advantages and
disadvantages of different churches
 • remaining separate
 • coming together?

3 Look at the symbol of the World Council of
Churches (**C**). Try to explain what it means.

4 Church leaders help people to understand
Christian beliefs and teachings. Work with a
partner to make a list of other influential
people who help to guide people in their
lives and beliefs. Explain the significance of
each. What is the value of such advice and
support? Think of situations in which you
might benefit from the knowledge and help
of an expert. Explain why in each case.

The Christian family at worship

The word 'church' has several meanings. It refers to the whole body of Christians. It also refers to particular groups of Christians; for example the Methodists are a church. 'Church' also refers to a building where Christians meet. There are many different kinds of church. By looking at different buildings we can learn about the ways in which Christians express their faith.

The first followers of Jesus met wherever they could, often in people's houses. A church does not require anything special – just a group of faithful believers. Some Christians today meet in each others' homes to pray. Such groups are called house churches. They can outgrow houses and some rent school halls or similar places to enable their members to meet. The worship is informal and no priest is involved.

A *The Bible is often placed on a decorative lectern for reading*

B *An Orthodox priest carries the Bible in an Easter process*

The Bible has a special place in the worship of all Christian groups. It has been translated into most languages and is read in the language of the community at worship. In both the **Anglican** and Roman Catholic Churches, there are readings from the Old and New Testaments in the service. The Bible is often placed on a symbolically decorative **lectern** (**A**). When the Gospel is read the congregation stands as a sign of respect. In Orthodox Churches, the Bible is often beautifully bound and treated with great reverence and respect. It is often carried in processions (**B**).

In many churches the service is based on the Bible reading. The theme of the reading is echoed in the choice of hymns and prayers. Members of the congregation may take their own Bibles to the service to follow the text. The preacher or visiting speaker's sermon may be based on the reading. He or she often stands in a **pulpit (C**). This is raised up so everyone can see the speaker. It is a way of showing how important the word of God is. The speaker uses all his or her expertise and energy to put across the teaching of the passage and to bring the words to life and make them meaningful.

Discussion question

After reading the next paragraph, discuss what you think is meant by the phrase 'offer themselves to Christ'.

Christians believe that the Holy Spirit is present in worship. In some churches, members of the congregation may be moved by the Holy Spirit during the service. They are invited to the front of the church to offer themselves to Christ. They are asked to pray a prayer of repentance by the minister.

THINGS TO DO

1 People often stand up as a sign of respect. Think of as many situations as you can in which it might be done.

2 Look at the photo of the lectern (**A**). It is not by chance that it is made in the form of an eagle with outstretched wings standing on a sphere. What do you think is the significance of this?

3 Using the photos in this unit to help you, write an article about the importance of the Bible for Christians in their worship. Unit 24 will also help you.

4 In this unit you have read about various Churches and some of the different features they have. Try to find out what sorts of churches there are in the area around your school and some information about them. You could make a display of your findings.

C *Preaching is often done from the pulpit in Christian churches so that all the congregation can see the speaker*

28 Bread and wine

Worship can take many forms. One important feature many denominations have in common is the sharing of bread and wine. Before he was arrested, Jesus shared a meal with his disciples (**A**). Many believe this was the Jewish **Passover** meal. At the supper, he broke a piece of bread and gave it to his disciples to eat. He also poured some wine and gave it to them to drink. These were signs of his promise of love and friendship. He said they should do this to remember him.

Different Churches share bread and wine in a variety of ways. In most there are prayers and readings in order to prepare the congregation. The bread and wine will be **consecrated** (made holy) or blessed. In the Roman Catholic, Orthodox and Anglican Churches the service is full of ceremony. Before taking part, people ask God to forgive their wrongdoings, selfishness and unkindness.

Discussion question

Why do you think people believe it is important to prepare themselves in this kind of way?

These Churches, in different ways, believe that Christ somehow becomes present in the bread and wine. How this happens is a mystery which cannot be fully explained.

The Roman Catholic service is called **Mass**. Anglicans call it **Holy Communion** or Eucharist. Until recently **lay** Roman Catholics received the bread (usually in the form of a wafer) whilst only the priests had wine as well. Now the laity often also receive wine. As the priests give the bread

A *Jesus sharing his last meal with his disciples before he was arrested*

wine takes place at least once each week.

In other denominations, including the Baptist and Methodist churches, this sharing may take place only once a month. Real bread is generally used and each person receives wine or grape juice in separate cups. The service is seen as a remembrance of Jesus' last supper rather than as a commemoration of his death. A plain table is used. Some Christian groups meet in their own homes to share bread and wine with no priest or minister present.

Some groups, for example the Society of Friends and the **Salvation Army**, do not have this service. However, for those who do it is always a very special occasion.

B *A Greek Orthodox priest giving bread and wine on a spoon as part of the Liturgy*

they say, 'The body of Christ', and as they give the wine they say, 'The blood of Christ'. The whole congregation shares one cup or **chalice**. In the Orthodox Church, where the service is called the **Liturgy**, people receive bread and wine together on a spoon (**B**). All three churches remember Jesus' death as a sacrifice which put right the relationship between human beings and God. They call the table on which the bread and wine are prepared an **altar** (**C**). Altars used to be places of sacrifice. The sharing of bread and

C *Bread and wine being prepared at the altar*

THINGS TO DO

1 In the Orthodox, Anglican and Roman Catholic Churches, sharing of the bread and wine is one of the **sacraments**. Sacraments are more than symbols, they are holy because it is believed God works through them. Design a chart or poster to illustrate and explain the meaning of the bread and wine in these Churches.

2 A regular family service in church will be a time of prayer and thanksgiving with hymns, Bible readings and a sermon. Design a short service. Choose or write prayers, hymns and readings on the theme of 'forgiveness'.

3 The Society of Friends and the Salvation Army do not have a service in which they share bread and wine. They say that every shared meal is an act of 'communion' or fellowship and should be treated as such. Why is sharing food with someone significant? On what special occasions is a meal shared? What are some of the differences between eating on your own and eating with others? Discuss this in class.

4 If your class were to have a friendship meal once a week with everyone bringing something, what problems might arise? How could they be dealt with? What good things might come from such a meal?

Living Christianity

When Jesus chose his disciples he said, 'Follow me'. Christians try to follow Jesus in their ordinary everyday lives.

Christian parents try to set a good example. They want to bring up their children knowing stories from Jesus' teaching and life. They encourage their children to get into the habit of praying. Some families say prayers before and after meals to thank God for his goodness (**A**).

Discussion question

What do you think it means for Christian parents to set a good example?

In some Christian families time may be put aside to study the Bible or pray together each week. Many believers read their Bible

daily to find guidance and encouragement from its teachings. Some may read it systematically from beginning to end. Others may open it at random. Christians can buy special notes which suggest passages for study and help to explain them.

Christians join with others in churches each Sunday for worship. Children may go to a Sunday school where they are taught more about the faith. Many people contribute to the life of the church by helping out in some way. They might serve coffee after the service, run a creche or help with the Sunday school or youth club. Others hold Bible study or prayer groups in their homes or maybe provide transport to church for the elderly.

Prayer is very important for Christians. This is the main way in which they communicate with God. Christians believe they can listen to God as well as speak to him. Very few ever expect to hear a voice actually speaking aloud to them. When they pray sincerely and thoughtfully they often find they can understand something better and feel they know what to do.

Prayer can take a number of forms. Christians like to praise God for his greatness and also thank him for all he has done. Somtimes they want to say sorry for wrongdoings. They confess what they have done and ask for forgiveness. This often helps them to make a new start and have the strength to put right what they have done wrong. Christians often ask for God's help either for themselves or others.

Some people question whether such prayers are answered. Many Christians accept that prayers can be answered in various ways. For example, someone may pray for a sick friend to be healed. The friend may seem to recover miraculously or she may find extra strength to bear the illness as a result of knowing that people care enough to pray for her. Prayer often shows Christians how they can help themselves with the situation they are praying about.

A *At mealtimes some families thank God for his goodness*

C *Some people prefer to sit for prayer*

B *Standing to pray*

The Lord's Prayer

'Our Father in heaven,
hallowed by your name,
your kingdom come,
your will be done,
on earth as in heaven.
Give us today our daily bread.
Forgive us our sins
as we forgive those who sin
against us.
Lead us not into temptation
but deliver us from evil.
For the kingdom, the power, and
the glory are yours,
now and forever. Amen.'

THINGS TO DO

1 Christians can stand, sit or kneel to pray (**B** and **C**). Sometimes they close their eyes. They might speak or sing prayers aloud or pray in silence. Think about and discuss the advantages of these different ways of praying. Write up your thoughts with illustrations.

2 Read the Lord's Prayer in the box. It is probably the most famous Christian prayer. It is often seen as a pattern for prayer because it contains four different forms: praise, thanksgiving, confession and petition (asking for things for ourselves and others). Draw a chart with a column for each of these four types of prayer. Divide up the Lord's Prayer and write each section in the correct column. Write your own prayer which includes all four forms.

3 Some churches have prayer lists. Anyone may write down something they would like people to pray about. What sort of things would you expect to find included? What might you choose to add and why?

4 Most Christians believe it is important to pass on their faith to their children. Imagine you are a parent. What ideas and beliefs are important enough to you for you to want to pass them on to your children? How do you think parents feel if their children reject their beliefs and follow other directions?

30

Faith and conviction

The majority of Christians put their faith into practice in their everyday lives and ordinary situations. Some are challenged by their faith to live in more unusual ways and dedicate themselves to causes they believe are important.

A few choose to dedicate their entire lives to God and join a **monastic order** of **monks** or **nuns**. In doing so, they take vows of poverty, chastity and obedience. This means they have no, or very few, personal possessions, they may not marry or have sexual relationships and their lives are lived in obedience to God. Some live entirely within their communities and devote their time to prayer, study and the work the communities do to support themselves. Members of other orders work in society. This is often in education, health care and in organizations which help the poor and underprivileged. These Christians aim to improve their own spiritual lives but also believe they help the world with their prayers and work (**A**).

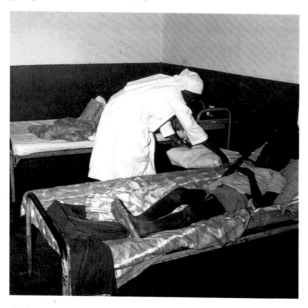

A *Many nuns work in the community*

Many Christians stress that Jesus spoke out strongly against injustice, poverty, greed and selfishness. They claim he did not only speak about how people could live a perfect life with God after their earthly lives are over. He also spoke about improving conditions in the world.

Christians often quote a passage from Luke's Gospel in which Jesus was reading from Jewish scriptures:

> '*The Spirit of the Lord is upon me, because he has chosen me to bring good news to the poor. He has sent me to proclaim liberty to the captives and recovery of sight to the blind; to set free the oppressed.*' (Luke 4:18)

They believe they should also take a stand against social injustice. A parable in Matthew's Gospel (25:31–46) is believed to make this challenge. The story tells of people being judged by whether they have fed the hungry, given a drink to the thirsty, received strangers into their homes, clothed the naked, taken care of the sick and visited those in prison. Jesus said:

> '*…whenever you did this for one of the least important of these brothers of mine you did it for me!… whenever you refused to help one of these least important ones, you refused to help me.*'

Discussion question

Do you think people have a responsibility to care for those who are less fortunate in society?

A Christian movement known as **Liberation Theology** started in South America to help the oppressed. Those who accept these ideals can now be found all over the world. A number have become well-known. Archbishop Desmond Tutu, for example, spoke out consistently about the evil of apartheid in South Africa (**B**). In Britain, the Church of England has spoken out in

B *Archbishop Desmond Tutu, who spoke out against apartheid in South Africa*

support of the homeless, unemployed and underprivileged. Its 1986 report, 'Faith in the City', criticized government policies of the time (**C**). Some people said Church and politics should not mix. Many Christians, however, believe these actions continue the work of Jesus in the world.

C *The Church of England report 'Faith in the City' called for action to help those in greatest need*

THINGS TO DO

1 Most people would not choose to live a life of poverty. Discuss the differences between the poverty of a monastic life and the poverty forced upon people who are underprivileged.

2 Some Christians work actively for improvements in society. What aspects of our society do you think need to be improved and how? Create a poster to illustrate your ideas. You might like also to find out about Christians who have actively tried to bring about social change.

3 Try to find out about how Christian groups in your area help in the community. Record the information on a chart.

4 St Paul wrote to the Christians in Corinth (1Corinthians 12:27) 'All of you are Christ's body, each one is a part of it.' Different parts of the body do different jobs. This and other chapters on Christianity in this book show that there are many ways of being a Christian. Write a short magazine article about how different Christians are like different parts of Christ's body. You could also illustrate the idea as a diagram, symbol or collage.

Islam: The word of Allah

31

Muslims believe that **Allah** (God) has given humankind guidance on how to live. He has communicated his message through his messengers and **prophets** to people in every age. According to the teachings of Islam, the final and most perfect revelation of the will of Allah is contained in the words of the holy **Qur'an** (**A**).

Muslims believe that every word of the Qur'an is the word of Allah. For Muslims it carries supreme authority. The words were revealed to the Prophet **Muhammad** by the angel **Jibril**. Muhammad recited them carefully to his followers. Every word was faithfully preserved and written down. Muslims believe that not one word has changed since they were first revealed to the Prophet Muhammad. This gives the Qur'an a unique authority in the eyes of Muslims.

A *A Muslim child reading from the Qur'an*

B *The beautiful and unique text of the Qur'an*

According to the Qur'an everyone has a choice about how they live. A person can go their own crooked way or they can follow the straight path that leads to peace. The Qur'an contains the guidance to take the right direction.

'And He commands you saying: This is my straight path, so follow it. Do not follow other paths, which will separate you from his path. Thus He has ordered you so that you may be truly obedient.' (6:153)

Discussion question

What path in life do you follow? Is it guided by any rules or teachings? Who is providing the signposts for your path in life?

The word Qur'an means 'recitation'. Its teachings cover every aspect of life – how to pray, what food to eat, how to run a business and how to govern a country. The laws and teachings of the Qur'an are not only for individuals but for the whole of society. Muslims believe it is the most complete revelation of the will of Allah.

The Qur'an is written in **Arabic**. The poetry and construction of the text is quite unique (**B**). Muslims say that when it is recited it has a special rhythm and beauty of sound that draws the listener to worship Allah.

The text of the Qur'an is divided into sections called **surahs**. The surahs are divided into verses. Muslim children learn to read the Qur'an in Arabic from an early age (**C**). This is the language in which the Holy Qur'an was first revealed to the Prophet Muhammad. There is a longstanding tradition of Muslims learning to recite the entire text of the Qur'an by heart. Muslims who can do this are called **hafiz**.

The Qur'an is handled with great care. Muslims always wash before they open its pages and cover their head as a sign of respect.

THINGS TO DO

1 Write a short conversation in which a Muslim describes the Qur'an and says why it is so important for them.

2 Imagine that a school like yours is given a very fine copy of the Qur'an for the library. Write a play in which a group of pupils ensure that it is kept in an appropriate place and treated with respect in the school library.

3 Listen to some recitations from the Qur'an. A selection can be heard in *The Life of the Last Prophet* by Yusuf Islam (formerly Cat Stevens), Mountain of Light Productions, P.O.Box 7404, London N7. After listening, in silence think about the sound of the words and the effect it has on you. Describe what you have heard and write down some of the words and thoughts that come to mind in response to the recitation.

4 Following your own path in life is encouraged in our society. 'Be yourself' and 'Do your own thing' are common expressions. Is this the right approach to life? Write a poem or a prayer which asks 'Which is the right way?'

C Children learn to read the Qur'an from an early age

32

Three key beliefs

The three most important beliefs in Islam are **tawhid** (Oneness of Allah), **risalah** (prophethood) and **akhirah** (life after death).

Muslims believe in One God Allah. Allah is unique. There is none like him. The belief in the Oneness of Allah is called tawhid and is essential to Islam. This is the teaching of the Qur'an:

> *'Say, He is Allah, the One. Allah is eternal and absolute. None is born of Him, nor is He born. And there is none like Him'* (112)

Allah is invisible and cannot be represented in any shape or form. Although Allah cannot be seen he can be described in terms of his attributes. These are the ninety-nine beautiful names of Allah (**A**). Allah is

A *The ninety-nine beautiful names of Allah*

B *A Muslim recites the ninety-nine beautiful names of Allah*

'All-Merciful' and 'All-Holy'. Muslims recite these names as an act of remembrance (**B**).

Meditating on the names of Allah is an important part of the **Sufi** tradition. Sufis are mystics who believe that the Oneness of Allah can be experienced in all aspects of life and in all creation (**C**).

According to the Qur'an, Allah has communicated his will through his prophets and messengers. This channel of communication between Allah and humankind is called risalah.

Discussion question

What do you understand by the word 'prophet'. A prophet is sometimes called a messenger. Do you think that this is a good definition?

Muslims accept the same prophets as we find in the Jewish and Christian scriptures. They accept Jesus as a prophet, but they reject the belief that he was the Son of God. According to the teachings of Islam, it is wrong to believe that anyone could be equal to or partner to God. Such a suggestion is **shirk**. It is a form of 'disbelief' because it suggests that Allah is not One.

Muslims believe that Muhammad was the last of the prophets. It was to him that Allah revealed the words of the Qur'an, his final and most complete revelation. Although Muslims believe that Muhammad's life was a perfect example for all to follow, they never regard him as divine.

Belief in life after death – akhirah – is very important to Muslims. Life on earth is a preparation for the eternal life to come. According to the Qur'an, there will be a **Day of Judgement** when everyone will be judged according to their deeds in this life. Those who have followed the teachings of the holy Qur'an will be rewarded in **Paradise**. But those who have ignored the will of Allah will be punished. Belief in akhirah is a strong influence in the life of a Muslim.

THINGS TO DO

1 Prepare a set of questions or a text with key words missing based on a summary of the main beliefs of Islam. Swap your work with a partner.

2 Those who believe in life after death often see this life as a time of preparation. Others say that it is not a dress rehearsal – we must live this life as best we can because it is the only one we have. What are the main differences between these points of view? Write a dialogue between a Muslim and someone who does not believe in life after death in which they discuss this question.

3 If there were to be another prophet what would you want their message to the world to be? Write your answers in the form of an e-mail or a letter to a Muslim friend who has told you about the Prophet Muhammad.

4 In what way do you think belief in life after death influences the lives of Muslims? If you believed in life after death would it affect how you lived your life? Discuss your answers in class. Write a report on the different points of view.

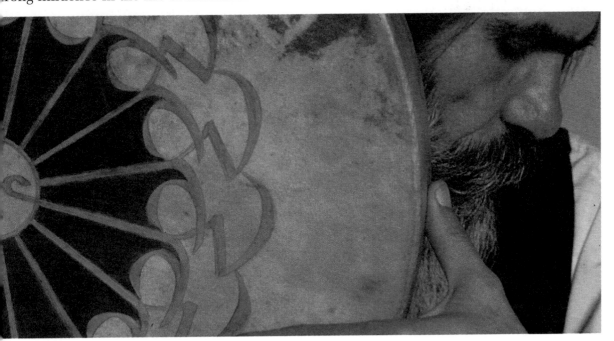

Th Sufi tradition emphasizes the oneness of all things. This is shown in their symbolism and art

33

Good examples

The life of a great leader or teacher is an inspiration to others. In Islam the word 'sunnah' means path or example. It refers to the example given in the life and sayings of Muhammad, which Muslims try to follow.

The collected sayings and stories from the life of Muhammad were carefully recorded and passed on. They are contained in the **Hadith**, which means 'information' or 'news'. It provides an important source for interpreting the teachings of the Qur'an. For example, the Qur'an requires Muslims to perform **salah**. The Hadith tells how Muhammad performed his prayers. It gives them more information on how to follow the teachings of the Qur'an.

Muslim children learn the stories in the Hadith (**A**). This is one for adults and children

'A man once asked the Prophet, "O messenger of Allah! Who deserves the best care from me?" The Prophet said, "Your mother." The man asked, "Who then?" The Prophet said, "Your mother." The man asked once again, "Who then?" The Prophet said, "Your mother."' (Hadith)

Every Muslim treasures these stories and sayings from the life of Muhammad.

Discussion question

What does this saying from the Hadith tell you about the place of women in Islam?

Muslims are also encouraged to learn from and follow the example of members of the

A *Muslim children study the Hadith at Madrasah*

There are two main groups of Muslims today. The **Sunni** and the **Shi'ah**. In most aspects of belief and practice there is no difference between them. However, they do have different views about who was the successor to Muhammad. Sunni Muslims believe that Abu Bakr, Muhammad's closest friend, was the first successor or Khalifah. Umar and Uthman who followed were also friends of Muhammad. The fourth Khalifah was Ali, the Prophet's son-in-law.

Shi'ah Muslims have a different view. Muhammad's daughter Fatimah and Ali had five children. Their son Husain is regarded by Shi'ah Muslims as the true successor to the Prophet. Husain was cruelly murdered when he was fighting to protect the weak from cruelty and oppression. Many Muslims remember Husain's martyrdom as an example of perfect self-sacrifice and faith (**B**).

Shi'ah Muslims re-enacting the martyrdom of Husain

Prophet's family. Khadijah is a role model for Muslim women. It was she who proposed marriage to Muhammad and became his wife. She lived with the Prophet for 25 years and was a great support to him. Muhammad and Khadijah had two sons and four daughters. Khadijah was the first person to accept that Muhammad was a Prophet and she believed that his message was from Allah. Her faith is an example to others.

THINGS TO DO

1 Write a conversation between a Muslim and a non-Muslim in which they talk about important role models or people who set a good example for others.

2 Design a cover for a copy of the Hadith. Remember that pictures of the Prophet are not permitted to avoid the risk of making idols. You should also avoid pictures of people or animals.

3 Khadijah had her own business. How does this challenge traditional ideas about women in Islam? Using the information in the text write and design a leaflet advertising a course on women in Islam which is intended to broaden people's view on the matter.

4 The story of Husain is re-enacted each year by Shi'ah Muslims. Is there a person who has shown great courage and self-sacrifice for whom you would suggest the events of their life should be re-enacted and remembered? Write your answer as a suggestion for a festival – to a newspaper or magazine. Describe how the events would be presented or acted out.

34

Belief in action

In Islam the word **ibadah** means worship or belief put into action. Muslims have been given rules for life called the Five Pillars through which they can put their faith into action.

The first is **shahadah**. This is a personal declaration of faith which states:

'I bear witness that there is no God except Allah, Muhammad is the Messenger of Allah.'

Shahadah reminds the believer that only Allah is to be worshipped, and this is an act of worship in itself.

The second pillar is salah, which is prayer. Muslims should pray five times a day (**A**). They can of course pray to Allah as often as they want but there are five set prayers. In this way Allah is remembered throughout the day.

The third pillar is **sawm**. This is fasting. Muslims must fast during the month of **Ramadan**, going without food or water during the hours of daylight. Muslims also refrain from sexual relations during the fast. Sawm involves the whole person – during this time ears, eyes, heart and hands must a refrain from evil. Fasting helps Muslims to build up the self-discipline and strength to resist evil in other aspects of their lives. It is an act of sacrifice to Allah, an act of worship

Zakah is the fourth pillar of Islam. Every Muslim must give two-and-a-half per cent of their savings to the poor and needy. Zakah is a part of Allah's plan to see that all members of the community are provided for. Muslims believe that everything in the world is a gift from Allah. It is the will of Allah that those who have wealth should share with those who have nothing. In this way they are following the example of Allah's generosity. Giving to the poor stops people from being too greedy and selfish and discourages feelings of envy and pride. Like fasting, zaka is an act of purification and self-sacrifice.

Discussion question

Why do you think that buying lottery tickets cannot count as zakah?

A *Muslim at prayer*

The Ka'bah at Makkah which pilgrims face as they pray to Allah

The last pillar of Islam is **hajj**. This is the pilgrimage to **Makkah (B)**. Muslims must try to go to the holy city at least once in their lifetime, if money and health allow. Hajj requires a person to give up worldly matters and to think only about Allah. It is an opportunity for Muslims to renew their faith and to join in worship with others from all over the world.

THINGS TO DO

1 Write three or four sentences on each of the Five Pillars of Islam. Explain the meaning of each. When you have done this, say what these five pillars all have in common.

2 Is there any point in having a belief or a commitment that does not show itself in action? Discuss this question in class. Write up the main points of the discussion. Include a Muslim point of view, explaining the importance of ibadah.

3 Design a board game in which the winner is the one who succeeds in fulfilling all five pillars.

4 The five pillars provide a framework that expresses the Muslim's belief. They remind the follower that there is a spiritual side to life and that they must serve the needs of others. The five pillars help them to learn from self-discipline and self-sacrifice. If you were to have five foundations on which to build your life what would they be?

35 Daily prayer

Discussion question

Salah is not always easy to perform at the given times. When might it be difficult?

The word 'salah' is often translated as prayer. However, it is not personal prayer but organized worship. It is a set of words and actions which focus the mind and body on Allah. Life is busy and it is hard to turn from the distractions of the world to concentrate on prayer. If a person wants to focus on Allah, they must put all other thoughts and desires to one side. The routine of salah helps the worshipper to achieve this.

Muslims are called to prayer five times a day – in the early morning, at noon, in the mid-afternoon, at sunset and last thing at night. The times are displayed for worshippers at the **mosque**. In Muslim countries the **adhan**, or call to prayer, reminds Muslims when it is time for salah. The **mu'adhin** calls the adhan from the minaret at the mosque.

Muslims remove their shoes before prayer. They must also wash in preparation for salah. This is called **wudu** (A). This action is not only to cleanse the body. It is also an opportunity to purify the heart and mind. The worshippers wash their feet, hands, face, mouth, nose and ears. As they do this, they remember the things they have said or done wrong and they prepare to stand before Allah, their maker.

Once the worshipper is ready, he or she expresses an intention to follow through a certain number of units of prayer. Each unit is called a **rak'ah**. It consists of words and positions. A rak'ah begins with the recitation of 'God is Great'. The words of salah are from the Qur'an and are recited in Arabic.

Muslims can pray at home or wherever they are at the set time. All they need is a clean place or a prayer carpet on which to

A *Muslims performing wudu in preparation for salah*

The prayer positions express total submission to Allah

THINGS TO DO

1 Write an information sheet on Muslim prayer that could be given to visitors to the mosque.
2 The following things are important in Islam. How are they expressed in salah:
   • submission
   • humility
   • concentration
   • purity
   • unity
   • sincerity
   • peace?
   Use the text and photos to help you write an answer for each point in the list.
3 Write up a discussion between two people with contrasting views – one who says it is best to pray alone and a Muslim who believes it is more beneficial to pray with others.
4 Du'a is an essential part of Muslim prayer. Either write a personal prayer that a Muslim your age might say at the end of salah *or* write a poem called 'Du'a' which expresses the deepest concerns and wishes a young person might have.

rostrate themselves. Muslims are encouraged to pray at the mosque whenever they can. Praying with others increases the benefit of salah. Worshippers stand or kneel shoulder to shoulder facing Makkah. This is a sign of equality. No one should try to stick out their chest in pride or try to separate themselves from their fellow worshippers. At the mosque the **imam** will often lead the prayer. The sound of the voices praying together and the movements of the prayer positions (**B**) express total submission to the will of Allah. There is a special atmosphere of peace and unity when Muslims pray together at the mosque.

When the set prayers have been completed, most Muslims stay to say their own personal prayers or **du'a** (**C**). They may ask forgiveness for the things they have done wrong. They may ask Allah to give them strength to overcome difficulties they face in life. They may also pray for their family, friends and loved ones.

C *The end of salah is often the time for personal prayers*

36

Home and family

Muslims believe that the family is the basis for building a good society. It should be in the home that children learn to love and respect others and to take responsibility for their behaviour. For most Muslims, the home is the place where the teachings of Islam are first learnt. Children follow the example of their parents and learn the pattern of salah (**A**).

According to the Qur'an there are different roles and responsibilities for men and women in the home. However the contribution of each is valued equally. The mother has the responsibility for bringing up the children and for teaching them the faith. That does not mean that Muslim women are not allowed to have a job or a career. In fact if a woman does go out to work, she is free to keep her earnings. It is the responsibility of the father to provide the financial support for his wife and children and other dependents. Islam place great emphasis on the importance of the family. Children must respect their parents and elders. Parents must be reasonable with their children. Elderly parents and relatives are cared for in the family.

A Children learn salah from the example of their parents

▶ *Muhammad told his followers they should share food*

The Qur'an requires all Muslims to dress modestly. Women should cover the whole body except for their face and hands when they are outside the family home. In the mosque most men wear a hat or cap for prayer and women have to wear a head covering.

The Qur'an also provides guidelines for eating and preparing food. The Qur'an forbids alcohol. It also forbids the following foods: carrion, i.e. animals that have died naturally, animals killed that have not had the name of Allah said over them, animals strangled to death, pigs, all meat-eating animals. All meat must be drained of blood. Food that is fit to eat is called **halal**. That which is forbidden according to Islamic law is called **haram**.

Discussion question

Everyone has rules about what they eat, how they eat and who they eat with. What are your rules?

Muhammad told his followers that they should share their food with others (**B**). At the festival of **Id-ul-Adha** every family that can afford it sacrifices an animal and shares the meat with the poor and needy. Diet varies from one Muslim home to another.

It will depend to some extent on family roots. However, the Qur'an encourages Muslims to eat food that is pure and good for the health. It also reminds Muslims to give thanks to Allah before eating.

THINGS TO DO

1 Imagine your best friend is a Muslim. You are staying with the family. Write a letter home explaining the way the Qur'an influences many different aspects of life in a Muslim home.
2 Design a leaflet on Muslim food laws. Include the teachings of Muhammad on meals and eating.
3 What are the particularly good things about the Qur'an's teaching on the family and home? What aspects of the teachings may Muslims find difficult to keep in the UK? Write up a balanced account of these issues making suggestions for ways in which any problems could be solved.
4 Every home and family is different. For example, Muhammad was brought up by his uncle. What makes a home a special place? You can write your answer in the form of a poem or a play or a story.

37

Place of prostration

The word mosque means a place of prostration. In the UK some mosques are converted houses. Many now are purpose-built with a dome and **minaret** (**A**). The minaret is traditionally the tower from where the mu'adhin calls the faithful to prayer. The dome is also a traditional part of the design. In warm climates it helps the air to circulate inside the mosque.

At the mosque there is always a place to wash before prayer. There is a prayer hall. It has no seating but the floor is carpeted. One wall, called the Qiblah, is marked with a niche to indicate the direction of Makkah. This is called the **mihrab**. There is also a platform from which the sermon is given on Fridays (**B**). In some mosques there is a gallery or a separate room for women. Most Muslim women choose to pray at home, especially when they are looking after young children. However, some mosques are now trying to encourage more women to attend for prayers.

At every mosque there is an imam. He usually leads the prayers but in fact any man can lead salah. The imam is elected by the community. He is not ordained but he is always a learned and respected man who knows the teachings of the Qur'an and can therefore offer advice and support to his community.

The Qur'an puts great emphasis on the value of good relations, friendship and community. Some mosques are community centres as well as places of worship. They may have facilities for a youth club, a kitchen and a reading room. Many mosques have classrooms where the children go to study the Qur'an. These mosque schools are called madrasahs.

Discussion question

What would you look for in a community? What makes a community more than just a group of people?

A *The traditional mosque has a minaret and dome*

B *Inside the mosque – the prayer hall*

At festival times Muslims have a sense of universal Ummah

The Qur'an calls on Muslims to make a special effort to attend the mosque for Friday **Jumu'ah** prayers. Jumu'ah prayers are held just after midday, when the imam gives a sermon. On Fridays the mosque is full and Muslims feel a sense of the larger Muslim community. Islam is a world-wide faith (**C**). The universal community of believers is called Ummah. Some Muslims try to go to a mosque bigger than their own for Jumu'ah prayers. At festival times Muslims try to travel to a centre where there is a large mosque. In this way, once or twice a year they will have a sense of the universal Ummah. Once in a lifetime they will try to go to Makkah for the hajj to pray with Muslims from all over the world (see page 71).

Muslims pray facing the direction of the **Ka'bah** in Makkah. This generates a sense of oneness and unity. Islam stresses the importance of the equality of all people. At the mosque Muslims from different ethnic, cultural and social backgrounds, stand shoulder to shoulder in prayer. All are equal in the eyes of Allah.

THINGS TO DO

1 Prepare a guide for a large mosque using diagrams, pictures and writing to help explain the design and function of the building.
2 Because of the prayer positions it is appropriate to have men and women praying separately and many mosques have a gallery for women. Design a poster that will encourage women to worship at the mosque at midday prayers once their children are old enough to go to school.
3 Write an illustrated page for a children's book on Islam that explains the meaning of the word Ummah. Say how the idea of Ummah comes across:
   • in prayer
   • in Jumu'ah prayers
   • at festival times
   • during the hajj.
4 Some people say that what is lacking in society is a sense of community. How could people build a greater sense of community belonging? Is there anything to learn from the Muslim model? Write an article for a local newspaper discussing these issues and making positive suggestions.

38

The Sikh scriptures

The Sikh holy book is called the **Guru Granth Sahib**. It contains the words and teachings of Guru Nanak (1469–1539) who was the first of the ten Gurus of the Sikh faith. It also contains the contributions of other Sikh Gurus. There are teachings from Hindu and Muslim holy men too. Sikhs believe that the words of the Guru Granth Sahib were revealed by God.

Discussion question

The Sikh holy book contains teachings from Muslims and Hindus as well as Sikhs. What does this tell you about Sikhism?

Guru Arjan (1563–1606), the fifth Guru, put together the first collection of all the hymns. He also included many of his own. He sang the words while his faithful follower, Bhai Gur Das, wrote them out. When the work was done, Guru Arjan encouraged his fellow Sikhs to listen to the teachings of the Gurus. He said they should show respect to the holy book, read it every day and act upon its teachings (**A**).

The tenth Guru, Guru Gobind Singh (1666–1708), saw that there would be no living Guru after him. He told the Sikh community that the Guru Granth Sahib would be like a living Guru for them in the future. Guru Gobind Singh was responsible for the final and complete version of the Guru Granth Sahib. Today the Guru Granth Sahib still represents the living word of the Gurus and is given the honour due to a living Guru.

A *Guru Arjan reading the Guru Granth Sahib*

The chauri is waved over the Guru Granth Sahib

The divine words revealed by the Gurus contained in the Guru Granth Sahib are called **Gurbani**. They are written in **Gurmukhi**. This was the script used by the Gurus to write Punjabi. The Guru Granth Sahib is written in poetry and structured into groups of lines according to Indian classical music. The poem is like a hymn and is called a shabad. This makes it easy to sing.

At the **gurdwara**, the Guru Granth Sahib is enthroned. It is read from a platform called a **takht**. In this way it is given a position of authority and respect. On the takht is a stool called the manji sahib. This is covered and cushioned to hold the holy book. There is usually a canopy over the scriptures. When the holy book is open a **chauri** is waved over the pages as a sign of respect (**B**).

The Guru Granth Sahib is read at all public acts of worship, festivals and celebrations. When worship is over, the Guru Granth Sahib is wrapped and carried reverently to a bed in a room of its own (**C**).

Guru Granth Sahib is the living Guru and therefore the sacred scriptures. However, there are other holy books for spiritual guidance, for example, the writings of the tenth Guru, known as **Dasam Granth**, the writings of Bhai Gurdas and the **Janamsakhis**, stories from the lives of the Gurus.

THINGS TO DO

1 Write a script for a TV or radio programme in which a Sikh being interviewed describes the place and importance of the Guru Granth Sahib. Make sure you bring out the idea of it being like a living Guru.

2 Using words and pictures, tell the story of the stages in the development of the Guru Granth Sahib. Make sure you include the following:
   • Guru Arjan's compilation of hymns
   • Guru Nanak, whose hymns make up an important part of the scriptures
   • Guru Gobind Singh and his message to Sikhs.

3 Do you know the words of your teachers by heart? Are you able to memorize paragraphs from books? Perhaps you know the words of certain songs and can join in when you hear them? Why do you think the Guru Granth Sahib is written the way it is? Write about a song which has meaning for you for which you know the words. Explain what it says and what it means to you.

4 Sikhs show reverence and respect for their holy book. Write a letter to a friend in which you describe how there are things to which you show reverence and respect.

C *The Guru Granth Sahib is put to bed*

39 Beliefs and teachings

Sikhs believe that there is only one God. They call God Waheguru, which means 'Wonderful Lord'. They also call God Sat Nam, the 'True Name'. God is without beginning and without end. There is no other like, or equal to, God. God is invisible. God is also everywhere and in everything and has no form or features.

According to the Guru Granth Sahib, God is a personal God who can be loved and worshipped (**A**). God's presence can be found within each of us. It is God who breathes life into every person. It is God's light that illumines the human soul and it is the presence of God that gives human beings their ability to judge between good and evil.

Discussion question

How does this Sikh concept of God compare with other ideas about God that you have met in your studies?

Sikhs believe that the soul is eternal. After death it enters another body and lives again. Sikhism teaches that we have lived many lives, passing through the animal kingdom on our way to being a human being. As humans we have the opportunity to become close to God. So we should live our lives according to the Gurus' teachings. In this way we can find union with God and release from the cycle of rebirth – this is called **mukti**.

Sikhs believe that all people are equal in the sight of God. This message is illustrated in the following story from the Janamsakhis.

A *God is a personal God who can be loved and worshipped*

B *Akbar the Great attending a langar at Ramgania Temple*

There was once a famous king of India called Akbar the Great (**B**). Akbar heard about the Sikh religion and planned to visit Guru Amar Das. He had heard that the Guru ran a **langar**, or community kitchen, where everyone was welcome. This was true. The Guru's langar never closed. Travellers, tramps, beggars and all who were hungry could come to eat there. Everyone sat together on the floor and was served a simple meal.

When the Sikhs heard that the king was coming they were very excited and began to think about special arrangements for his visit. But Guru Amar Das stopped them. He thought carefully. The king was a human being like any other visitor to the langar. So when Akbar the Great arrived he took his meal in the langar with the common people and ate the simple food provided.

The king was so impressed with the Guru's langar he offered him a royal grant. Guru Amar Das thanked him for his offer but he could not accept. The langar must be run on the earnings of ordinary people. That way everyone would feel equal and no one would be regarded as an outsider.

THINGS TO DO

1 Write a talk on Sikh beliefs about God to be used for 'Thought for the Day' on the busy morning radio news programme.
2 Tell the story of the King and the Guru in words and pictures as if for a story book for Sikh children.
3 Does every person have a sense of right and wrong? Where do you think people get their sense of morality? Discuss these questions in class. Write a conversation between a Sikh and non-Sikh on the question of the human conscience.
4 The story of Akbar the Great is a powerful reminder of the real meaning of equality. Write your own story to illustrate this belief that all people are equal.

Principles to live by

There are three principles that guide Sikh living. Nam Simran or Nam Japna, which means remembering God at all times, **Kirat karna**, which means earning an honest living, and Vand Chhakna, which means sharing with others who are less fortunate.

Nam Simran is the remembrance of God. This is the basis of all Sikh worship and life. There are many ways to do this. It may mean singing hymns of praise or meditating on the name of God or reciting the scriptures. Through these acts of remembrance the heart and mind become filled with awareness of the presence of God. Most people are full of selfish desires and cling to the material world. The aim of the Sikh is to become God-filled.

Sikhs do not believe that you have to shut yourself away from everyday life and work to find God. The idea of the ascetic alone in the forest and begging for alms is rejected by the Gurus. Sikhs are required to earn their living by honest means (Kirat Karna). They must be a part of the real world of work, raising a family, and running a home. God can be found in every aspect of life – even in the workplace.

Discussion question

What work might be included in 'earning a living by honest means'? What sort of work does it rule out?

There was once a wealthy man called Malak Bhago. He made a fortune but he showed his workers no mercy and paid them poor wages. The fame of Guru Nanak reached him. So he sent out an invitation for the

A *Guru Nanak squeezing the bread*

Sikhs share their resources – Van Chhakna

Guru to come to his house to eat. Guru Nanak chose instead to accept the hospitality of Lalo, a poor carpenter.

Malak Bhago wanted to know why Guru Nanak had preferred the poor man's bread to his fine meal. Guru Nanak put out his hand and asked him for a piece of bread from his table. In the other hand, Guru Nanak held the bread from the table of Lalo. He then squeezed the two pieces of bread (**A**). From Malak Bhago's bread came drops of blood and from the poor man's came pure sweet milk. Then Guru Nanak said that he preferred bread that was earned by honest means and hard work to bread that was earned at the expense of the blood and suffering of others.

The third guiding principle for Sikhs is Van Chhakna, which means sharing your resources with others (**B**). This is not just about giving away money to charity. It can mean finding time to visit the sick and lonely or using one's skills – to help with repairs at the gurdwara, for example.

THINGS TO DO

1 Write a summary of the three principles that guide the Sikh way of life. Use the correct vocabulary. Do you think that these are a sound basis for a good life? Give your answer with reasons.

2 The religious path in life is not always easy. Look again at the three principles described in the text. What problems do you think the Sikh might meet in trying to fulfil these three principles in the UK?

3 Tell the story of Guru Nanak and the two pieces of bread in the form of a cartoon strip. Say what the message of the story is for Sikhs.

4 Why do you think the rich man wanted to meet Guru Nanak? If Guru Nanak were alive today, which 'fat cats' would come up against his criticism? Write an article for a Sikh newspaper which relates the issues in the story to the world today.

41 Worship

Sikhs believe that learning to put God rather than yourself at the centre of life is hard. It becomes easier when you are part of a community where others are on the same quest. The Sikh community at the gurdwara is called the **sadhsangat.** The sadhsangat is where remembrance of God, working and sharing with others are all combined to provide the right environment for the spiritual and moral growth of the individual. There is no priesthood in the sadhsangat. All are equal. The community elects a management committee to run the gurdwara. This in turn appoints a **granthi** to lead the worship.

Discussion question

How does the life of the community around you influence what you believe and the way you think and act?

The life of the sadhsangat is centred around the gurdwara. Gurdwara means door or house to the Guru. The main room of the gurdwara is the prayer hall where the Guru Granth Sahib is installed and where diwan or public worship is held. Sikhs wash before arriving at the gurdwara and on entering they remove their shoes. They also cover their heads in the presence of the Guru Granth Sahib. When Sikhs enter the prayer hall they first bow before the Guru Granth Sahib and leave a gift of food or money.

Worship begins with **kirtan**. These are hymns from the Guru Granth Sahib. The worshippers stand with hands folded for a prayer called the **ardas**. They remember God, the Gurus and those who have given their lives for the faith. They repeat God's name Waheguru, 'Wonderful Lord'. The prayer ends with a blessing for all humanity. The congregation sits for the reading from the Guru Granth Sahib (**A**). The reader carefully lets the pages fall open at random

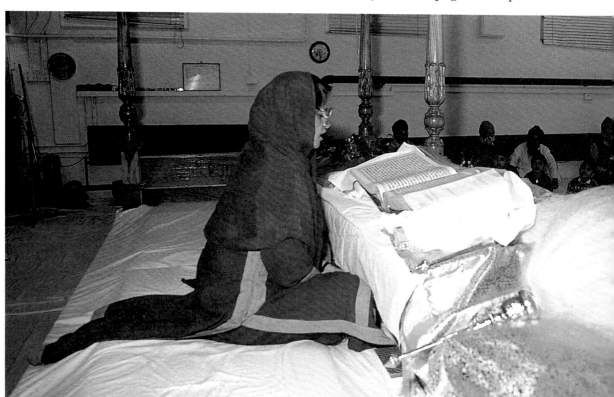

A Reading from the Guru Granth Sahib

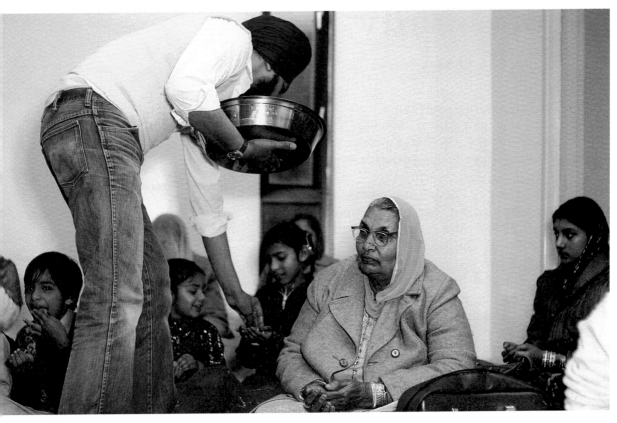

B *The serving of karah parshad at the end of a service*

and recites one shabad. This is the Guru's guidance for the day. These words are from a hymn from the Guru Granth Sahib:

> *'Let him who is known as a Sikh of the Guru rise early and ponder God's name. Arising from sleep as the new day is breaking he washes his body and cleanses his soul. Repeat the Lord's name as the Guru commands us, for thus our sins are washed away; So greet every dawn with the words of the Guru and utter God's name through the length of the day.'*

At the end of the service, **karah parshad**, a sweet mixture made from flour, butter, sugar and water is offered before the Guru Granth Sahib. When it has been blessed, it is served to everyone present (**B**).

THINGS TO DO

1 Write a guide to Sikh worship at the gurdwara for a visitor who knows nothing about Sikhism. Provide enough information so that they know what to expect when they go to the service.

2 Design a card or leaflet which invites new Sikhs in the area to visit their local gurdwara and which reminds them of the importance of the sangat.

3 Look at the hymn from the Dasam Granth. Use words from the text in an article on Sikhism for a local newspaper.

4 Karah parshad is sweet. It represents the blessing of God. Food is often a symbol of spiritual nourishment. We talk about food for thought. Sikhs believe the human spirit is hungry and needs nourishment. In what ways can you feed the spirit? In what ways is the spirit hungry? Write a poem or prayer in which these ideas and questions are explored.

42 Community meal

The Sikh community gives the impression of being like a large family. The worshippers pray together; they also cook and eat together. Every gurdwara has a langar or kitchen. After worship the congregation shares a community meal. This is also called langar. When they come to the gurdwara, worshippers bring gifts of food and money. So the gurdwara is able to provide food free to visitors. Each week a family or several families volunteer to provide and prepare the langar (**A**). This can be a major undertaking as there may be several hundred people to feed.

In the langar everyone sits together and eats the same meal (**B**). The food provided is vegetarian. In this way everyone can eat the same food. Men and women are involved in

B *Eating together in the langar*

the cooking and serving of the meal. Langar is a demonstration of equality. In India the caste system used to prevent people from different social backgrounds eating together. The Sikh langar offered a way of breaking down the barriers of caste and the divisions of wealth and poverty. No one is turned away from the langar.

A *Sikhs preparing the langar in India*

C Gurdwaras provide hospitals and schools and serve the local community, such as this one in Kenya, which runs a large school

Discussion question

What kind of community events bring people of different backgrounds and social classes together?

The gurdwara is open to everyone. It has always been a centre for serving the community at large. In India and Africa some gurdwaras provide hospitals, schools and charity programmes (**C**). In the UK, the gurdwara is a community centre. Many gurdwaras run a senior citizens club and provide transport for the elderly in the community. The gurdwara may also have a youth club and run classes where young people can learn to read Punjabi or to sing hymns and play a musical instrument – the tabla or harmonium. Involving young people in the life of the sadhsangat is considered very important. It ensures that the traditions and values of the faith can be passed on to the next generation.

The gurdwara is the main centre for all religious occasions. Naming ceremonies, weddings and funeral rites all take place here. The gurdwara is managed by a committee which is elected by the congregation. Committee members are volunteers who give up their time to serve the community.

Volunteers also help with the langar, the language classes, the cleaning, transport and repairs. People bring their different skills to contribute to the life of the sadhsangat.

THINGS TO DO

1 Give an account of the Sikh langar and its contribution to the life of the community. Write it in the style of an article for a local newspaper in an area where a new gurdwara has been set up.

2 Design a poster calling for volunteers to help at the gurdwara – think of all the different tasks that need to be carried out. Remind people of the teachings of the Gurus. (Unit 40 might help you with this.)

3 Imagine that someone in your family has been invited by a Sikh friend to join them for langar at the gurdwara. They do not know anything about Sikhism and ask you all about it. Write a conversation in which you explain what will happen and what it means.

4 Food brings people together in lots of ways. A shared meal can be a sign of friendship and trust. Write an account of an occasion when sharing a meal has brought friendship and trust or brought people together. If you cannot think of an actual occasion write an imaginary one.

43

In the home

Sikhs believe that God is to be found in the ordinary routines of daily life. There is no need to give up work or leave home and become a recluse to find God. Every action can become an act of worship if it is carried out in God's name. No task is considered unclean or unworthy as long as it is honest and causes no harm.

A *A Sikh family praying together at home*

Devout Sikhs rise early in the morning when the world is quiet. They shower before reciting their prayers (**A**). This prayer, the japji, is from the words of Guru Nanak:

'Let every tongue become a hundred thousand; let each be multiplied twice ten times more. Let this multitude of tongues then join together, each repeating a hundred thousand times the name of creation's Lord. This path is a stairway leading to the Master, an ascent to the bliss of mystical union. All may follow it, even the lowliest, if they but heed the word from above.' (Japji 32)

Some Sikhs drop in at the gurdwara on their way to work. Others may stop on their way home. They try to keep God in mind constantly. They may recite hymns and prayers from the scriptures when doing daily routine tasks. Only a few Sikh families have a copy of the Guru Granth Sahib at home as it must have a room of its own. Most Sikhs have a prayer book which contains a selection of hymns from the scriptures.

Discussion question

What might be the different points of view represented in a Sikh family discussing whether to purchase a copy of the Guru Granth Sahib for their home?

Food in the Sikh home varies from one family to another (**B**). Many Sikhs choose to be vegetarian although there is no clear requirement for this. However, Sikhs do not eat halal meat that has been slaughtered in the Muslim tradition. Alcohol is forbidden, as are all other strong intoxicants, particularly smoking. Guru Nanak said that Sikhs should only become intoxicated by love for God.

Sikhs are encouraged to marry and raise a family. It is through family life that a person learns to love. This is an important step in learning to love God and serve others. Often

3 *Sharing food is important in Sikh family life*

men and women go out to work. Grandparents may live with the family and help to bring up the children. Children learn to practise their faith from the example of their elders. They are also told the stories of the Gurus. Education is regarded as important in Sikhism and children are encouraged to work hard at school.

THINGS TO DO

1 Show the difference between the day in the life of a non-religious person and the day in the life of a Sikh by using two diagrams. You could use circles to represent the hours of the day or simple time charts down the page.

2 Design a poster explaining the teachings and rules for living which influence the home life of the Sikh

3 Is love something that is learnt or does everyone have a natural tendency to love? What kind of environment or way of life can help people be more loving towards others? Discuss these questions in class. Write up your answers, taking account of the ideas of others.

4 Sikhs believe that we must protect the rights of people to hold to their religious beliefs and practices. Write a declaration of rights for your school regarding religious beliefs and practices. Explain your declaration and why it is needed.

44

Service to others

Sikhs believe that the soul survives death and takes on a life in a new body. If a person's actions are good they will move closer to God in the next life. If their actions are evil or selfish they will move further away from God. By following the teachings of the Gurus, Sikhs hope to find union with God and liberation from the cycle of rebirth (mukti). Some Sikhs achieve this liberated state of bliss in this life. They live only to work for the good of others.

All Sikhs try to serve others in their daily lives. Service is called **sewa**. It helps to purify the soul. It is also an important example to others. Sikhs offer their service in various ways (**A**). They may help at the gurdwara, they may visit the sick or raise funds for charity. Sikhs are encouraged to give as much as they can to those in need. Guru Amar Das said they should try to give a tenth of their savings towards the service of the community. This is called **Daswand**.

B *Namdhari Sikhs wear homespun cloth as a sign of simplicity, purity and humility*

A *Sikhs cleaning the pavement outside the Golden Temple, Amritsar*

Discussion question

What do you understand by the word 'service'. Suggest examples of people in your community whose lives are based on service to others.

Sikhs should not make a show of their service or giving. Namdhari Sikhs place great importance on simplicity and service. They believe that the line of Gurus continued after Guru Gobind Singh. According to their twelfth Guru, a Sikh must always conceal his good deeds from others. Many Namdhari Sikhs wear clothes from white homespun cloth as a sign of simplicity, purity and humility (**B**).

Sewa is not just a matter of looking after the people we love. It means serving those in need no matter who they are. This is illustrated in the following story.

Guru Gobind Singh and his men were in battle against the Emperor Aranguzeb. The Sikhs were surrounded. Men from both sides of the conflict lay wounded and dying in the field. The battle was hard and Guru Gobind Singh's men were tired. In the distance they could see a man bending down giving water to the wounded. It was a Sikh called Bhai Khanaya. When they looked again they saw that he was giving water to the enemy soldiers as well as to the Sikhs. The men complained to their Guru that Bhai Khanaya was helping the enemy. Guru Gobind Singh called Bhai Khanaya to him. 'Is it true?' he asked. 'Yes' said Bhai Khanaya. 'Many of these men are dying; the least I can do is give them water.' Guru Gobind Singh proclaimed that Bhai Khanaya was a true and faithful Sikh as all followers must serve the needy no matter who they are (**C**).

THINGS TO DO

1 Explain the Sikh teaching on sewa using words and pictures to show its meaning.
2 Design a badge or symbol which represents a life of simplicity, purity and humility. Explain the symbol in writing.
3 Write up the story of Bhai Khanaya as a play for the classroom. Make sure you bring out the meaning of the tale.
4 We often want people to know about our good deeds and it is hard to keep quiet about them. Why is this? Is a good deed better if we do not boast about it? Write a story or a play in which someone carries out a really good deed. They do not let anyone know that they were responsible and so receive no recognition.

C Sikhs providing water for thirsty visitors at the Golden Temple, Amritsar

45 Unity and diversity

In each religious tradition there is both unity and diversity. That is to say, the believers all share certain important beliefs or practices but there are differences too. For example, all Christians accept Jesus Christ as their Lord and Saviour, no matter which of the various Churches they belong to. It may be the holy book that unites people of the same faith. For example, all Jews look to the Torah (**A**) as the word of God and regard it as their guidebook for life.

The unity of a religion may be reinforced through shared practices. For example, salah (**B**) is the same for Muslims all over the world. It may also be the roots of a

B *Salah unites Muslims all over the world*

religion that gives it its unity, such as with Hindus, who all look back to India as the cradle of their faith. In these ways we are able to see common beliefs within a faith. Without any unity there would be no specific religion to recognize. There would just be a lot of different people believing and doing a lot of different things.

Discussion question

What other aspects of a religion unite the believers of it?

There are also things that bring about diversity, or differences, in a religion. Sometimes there is diversity in the way people interpret their scriptures. For example, the main difference between Orthodox and Reform Jews is the way they interpret the Torah.

A *The scrolls of the Torah*

There may be diversity in the way people ractise their faith. For example, some lindus approach God through daily worship at a shrine, others through yoga nd meditation.

The differences within a religion may be ue to the climate, culture or the politics of where the followers live. Buddhists living n the UK, for example, would not be able to ely on the daily alms round for their food, whereas Buddhists in Thailand are rovided for by the lay community (**C**).

Differences in belief or practice within religion can sometimes cause bitterness r even conflict. However, shared beliefs nd common ground between different roups gives a religion an identity and nity that can hold the faith together espite these internal differences. Some say hat diversity within a religion is a healthy ign. It shows that the needs of different eople are being met and that the religion s alive and kicking! In the six religions epresented in this book there is evidence of oth unity and diversity.

C *The Buddhist alms round in Thailand*

Glossary

A

Abraham first well known Jewish person. Muslims also respect him as a prophet and a worshipper of Allah

Adhan call to prayer

Akhirah life after death

Aleinu important Jewish prayer at the end of each service

Allah the Islamic name for God

Alms charity, gift of food

Altar name given to the table used in some Christian denominations during the service in which bread and wine are shared

Anglican churches linked to the Church of England which are part of the Anglican communion

Anicca impermanence. Buddhist teaching that nothing remains unchanged

Arabic the language of the holy Qur'an

Ardas Sikh formal prayer offered at most religious occasions

Arjuna one of the five Pandava brothers in the story of the Mahabharata

Ark focal point of the synagogue, containing Torah scrolls. Also called Aron Hakodesh

Artha economic development, material success

Arti welcoming ceremony involving the offering of light

Asceticism self discipline through giving up comforts and pleasures of life

Ashkenazim Jews who trace their ancestors through Eastern and Central European communities

Atman soul

Avatar down coming, one who descends, descent of a deity

B

Bhagavad Gita sacred Hindu scriptures, The Song of the Lord, the words of Krishna

Bhakti yoga the way of loving devotion, one of the paths to moksha

Bhikkhu fully ordained Buddhist monk

Bhikkhuni fully ordained Buddhist nun

Bible name given to the holy scriptures of the Christian faith. Jews sometimes use the name to refer to their scriptures too

Bimah raised platform for reading the Torah in a synagogue

Bishops high ranking leaders of the Christian Church

Bodhisattva one who puts off becoming a buddha in order to help other living beings

Brahman Universal Spirit, Ultimate Reality, God

Brahmin priest, priesthood

Buddha enlightened being

C

Canon accepted books of the Bible

Cardinals high ranking leaders of the Roman Catholic Church

Chalice cup or goblet used to hold wine in a Christian service in which bread and wine are shared

Challot plural of Challah. Enriched bread used particularly on Shabbat and during Jewish festivals

Chauri symbol of authority, a fan waved over the Guru Granth Sahib as a sign of respect

Church of England the established Church in England

Consecrated to make sacred or holy with a blessing by a priest

Creeds summary statements of religious beliefs

D

Dasam Granth collection of hymns from the Tenth of the Sikh Gurus

Daswand one-tenth of a Sikh's savings given to charity

Day of Judgement the last day at the end of time when God will raise the dead and everyone will be judged according to their deeds

Deity god or goddess

Denominations different branches of the Christian Church

Dhamma ultimate truth. The teachings of Gotama Buddha

Dharma religious duty, law, what is right

Disciples followers or learners taught by a teacher: in a Christian sense, followers of Jesus Christ

Du'a personal prayer

E

Ecumenical Movement movement within the Christian Church towards co-operation and eventual unity

Eightfold Path Gotama Buddha's eight-point guidelines for putting an end to suffering

Elders religious leaders in some Christian denominations

Enlightenment liberation from the bonds of earthly life

F

Four Noble Truths Gotama Buddha's teaching which explains why life is as it is

G

Gemara commentary on the Mishna (written version of the oral tradition of Judaism) included in the Talmud

Ghee lamp lamp which burns on clarified butter (ghee), used in Hindu worship

Gospels 'good news'. Name given to the books in the Bible which tell about the life of Jesus Christ

Granthi someone who reads the Guru Granth Sahib and officiates at Sikh religious ceremonies

Gurbani divine word revealed by the gurus

Gurdwara Sikh place of worship

Gurmukhi script of the Punjabi language in which the Guru Granth Sahib is written

Guru spiritual teacher, religious teacher

Guru Granth Sahib Sikh holy scriptures

H

Hadith the sayings of the Prophet Muhammad

Hafiz someone who knows the whole Qur'an by heart

Hajj annual pilgrimage to Makkah

Halal anything that is permitted under Islamic law, e.g. permitted foods

Haram anything that is not permitted under Islamic law

Havdalah ceremony marking the end of Shabbat

Holy Communion a name given to the service in which Christians share bread and wine

I

Ibadah acts of faith, e.g. worship, faith in action

Id-ul-Adha festival of sacrifice

Iman leader, a person who leads prayer at the mosque

Incense substance burnt for its sweet scent, used in worship

Israel the world-wide community of Jews; the land of Israel; the modern state of Israel founded in 1948

J

Jacob one of the sons of Isaac. Understood to be father of the people of Israel

namsakhis stories about the Gurus, especially Guru Nanak

ti caste, social group based on occupation

ril in Islam name for the angel Gabriel

ana yoga the way of knowledge, one of the paths to moksha

mu'ah Friday prayers at the mosque when a sermon is given

K

a'bah the sacred house of God in Makkah, focus of Muslim pilgrimage

ama sense enjoyment, one of the four aims in life in Hindu tradition

amma intentional actions that affect one's circumstances in this and future lives

arah Parshad blessed food shared out at Sikh worship

arma deeds, actions, the effects of actions

arma yoga the way of action, one of the paths to moksha

ddush a Jewish prayer used to make the Shabbat and festival days holy. It is usually recited over wine

ngdom of God an ideal of Christian life. Some believe it to be a new life Christians have after death and others think it can be experienced in this life

ppah head covering worn by Jews during prayers, Torah study etc. Some Jews wear it all the time

irat Karna earning an honest living by one's own efforts

irtan Sikh devotional singing, hymns

osher fit, proper. Foods allowed by Jewish dietary laws

rishna an avatar or manifestation of the God Vishnu, many Hindus see Krishna as the supreme manifestation of God

rishna Conciousness Movement Hindu reform movement based on the teachings of the saint Chaitanya in which Krishna is worshipped as Supreme Lord

shatriya warrior and princely class, one of the four classes of Hindu traditional society

L

aity lay people. The ordinary men and women of a religious community who are not priests or monks or nuns

Langar kitchen where food is prepared at the Gurdwara, also means the community meal

Laws of Manu Hindu scriptures giving teaching on dharma

Lay ordinary men and women of a religious community who are not priests or monks or nuns

Lectern stand supporting the Bible

Liberation Theology a Christian movement actively dedicated to stamping out social injustice

Liturgy name given in the Orthodox Church to the service in which bread and wine are shared

M

Mahabharata Hindu scriptures from the smriti tradition one of the great epic stories

Mahayana 'great way'. A main form of Buddhism in which belief in Bodhisattvas is important

Makkah (sometimes known as Mecca) the holy city where the Ka'bah is and where Muhammad was born

Mala a string of 108 beads used by Buddhists in prayer or meditation

Mandir Hindu temple containing a shrine to a deity

Mantra a chant used for worship and meditation

Mass name given to the service in which bread and wine are shared in the Roman Catholic Church

Maya the created world which changes and has no lasting reality

Meditation the control and discipline of the mind which may involve reflection, concentration, deep thought and being still

Merit spiritual reward for certain good works and attitudes

Messiah Hebrew word meaning 'anointed one' or 'king'

Metta loving kindness

Mihrab niche in mosque wall indicating direction of Makkah

Minaret tower of a mosque from where call to prayer is given

Ministers religious leaders in some Christian denominations

Minyan ten males over the age of 13, required for a service in many synagogues. Some Jewish communities may include women in this number and others do not even require a minyan for a service

Mishnah first written form of the oral tradition of Judaism

Moksha liberation from the cycle of karma and samsara, union with God

Monastic order religious group living life of poverty, chastity and obedience to God

Monks religious men living lives of poverty, chastity and obedience to God

Mosque place of prostration, Muslim place of worship

Mu'adhin one who calls the faithful to prayer

Muhammad the last and final prophet sent by Allah to give his message to humankind. Whenever Muslims mention his name they add the words 'peace be upon him'. When written this is sometimes shortened to 'pbuh'

Mukti liberation from the cycle of rebirth, union with God

Murtis images used in worship in Hindu temple

N

Ner Tamid the light always burning above the Aron Hakodesh in a synagogue

New Testament collection of 27 books which form the second section of the canon of the Christian scriptures

Nibbana 'blowing out'. A state of perfect peace in which greed, hatred and ignorance are no longer experienced. Buddhist word for liberation from the bonds of earthly life

Nicene Creed a statement of beliefs recited in many churches

Nuns religious women living lives of poverty, chastity and obedience to God

O

Old Testament part of the canon of Christian scriptures which is shared with Jews. It has 39 books and was originally written in Hebrew

Orthodox Church those branches of the Christian Church which are traditionally found in Russia, Greece and Eastern Europe

Orthodox Judaism teaches that traditional Jewish practices are important

P

Pali Canon the scriptures used by Theravada Buddhists written in the Pali language

Paradise heaven, where the faithful are promised a place after death if they have followed the will of Allah

Passover one of the three 'pilgrim' festivals of Judaism. Celebrated in Spring it commemorates the Exodus from Egypt. Also called Pesach

Pope the head of the Roman Catholic Church, sometimes called the Bishop of Rome

Priests religious leaders

Prophet someone sent by God to speak God's message

Prostrate bow down to the ground in prayer

Pulpit a raised platform from which sermons are preached

Purana Hindu scriptures from the smriti tradition containing stories about the deities

Q

Qur'an The Muslim holy book, the word of Allah

R

Rabbis ordained Jewish teachers. Often the religious leaders of Jewish communities

Rak'ah a cycle of prayer in Muslim salah

Ramadan Muslim month of fasting

Ramayana Hindu sacred scriptures from smriti tradition, one of the epics, story based on the life of Rama

Rebirth being born into a new life

Reform Judaism teaches that Jewish beliefs and practices can be altered to suit changes in people's lifestyles

Risalah prophethood, channel of communication between Allah and humankind

Roman Catholic Church part of the Christian church led by the Bishop of Rome or Pope

Rupa image of the Buddha

S

Sacraments outward signs of inward blessings

Sadhsangat Sikh congregation of worshippers, the true congregation

Salah Muslim set prayer said five times a day. One of the Five Pillars of Islam

Salvation Army branch of the Christian Church founded by William and Catherine Booth

Samsara the cycle of rebirth

Sangha 'community'. Sometimes the word is used of the community of

Buddhist monks (bhikkhus) and nuns (bhikkhunis) and sometimes of the whole Buddhist community

Sawm fasting from dawn to sunset. One of the Five Pillars of Islam

Scribe person who hand writes scrolls of Torah

Sefer Torah Torah scroll. The five books of Moses hand-written on parchment and rolled to form a scroll

Sephardim Jews who trace their ancestors through Mediterranean communities, particularly Spain, North Africa and the Middle East

Sewa unselfish service to others

Shabbat Jewish weekly holy day which starts at sunset on Friday and ends at nightfall on Saturday

Shahadah Muslim declaration of faith

Shema an important Jewish prayer from the Torah which expresses a clear belief in one God

Shi'ah followers, Muslims who accept Ali as successor after death of the prophet Muhammad

Shirk unbelief, wrong belief, belief that Allah has an equal or a partner or son

Shrine place where worshippers make offerings usually containing an image of a god or goddess

Shruti 'revealed', collection of the most ancient and sacred of Hindu scriptures including the Vedas

Shudra servant class, one of the four classes in traditional Hindu society

Simchat Torah festival celebrating the completion and beginning again of the cycle of the weekly Torah reading

Smriti 'remembered', collection of Hindu scriptures including the Mahabharata and Ramayana

Society of Friends branch of the Christian Church often known as Quakers

Sufi mystic in Muslim tradition which emphasizes the oneness of God and the oneness of all things.

Sunni Muslims who accept Abu Bakr as the successor after the death of Muhammad

Surah verse or division of the Qur'an

Synagogue building for Jewish public prayer, study and meeting

T

Takht platform in gurdwara from which the Guru Granth Sahib is read

Tallitot plural of tallit. Four-cornered garment with fringes worn by many Jewish men at some times of prayer

Talmud Mishnah and Gemara collected together

Tawhid belief in the Oneness of Allah

Ten Sayings Ten rules or sayings from the Torah. Also called Ten Commandments

Tenakh the collected 24 books of the Jewish Bible

Thanka Buddhist painting of buddhas, religious symbols and symbolic scenes

Theravada 'way of the elders'. A main form of Buddhism developed in Sri Lanka and South East Asia

Three Jewels Buddha, Dhamma and Sangha

Tipitaka 'three baskets'. The three parts of the Buddhist Pali scriptures

Torah law or teaching. The five books of Moses

U

Untouchables a title given to groups in traditional Hindu society who were regarded as outside the four main classes

Upanishads ancient Hindu scriptures belonging to the shruti tradition

V

Vaishya merchant class, one of the four main classes in traditional Hindu society

Vajrayana a form of Buddhism mainly found in Tibet and India

Varnas four main classes of traditional Hindu society

Vedas the most ancient and sacred of Hindu scriptures belonging to the shruti tradition

Vicars name given to priests of parishes in the Church of England

Vishnu one of the three main aspects of God in Hinduism, God as Preserver

W

Wudu Muslim ritual washing before prayer

Y

Yad hand-held pointer used when reading the Sefer Torah

Yoga discipline of mind, body and life

Z

Zakah giving to the poor and needy, one of the Five Pillars of Islam